Something in Common

HARVARD EDUCATION LETTER
IMPACT SERIES

The *Harvard Education Letter* Impact Series

The *Harvard Education Letter* Impact series offers an in-depth look at timely topics in education. Individual volumes explore current trends in research, practice, and policy. The series aims to bring many voices into the conversation about issues in contemporary education, and to consider reforms particularly from the perspective of—and on behalf of—educators in the field.

Other books in this series:

I Used to Think . . . And Now I Think . . .
Edited by Richard F. Elmore

Inside School Turnarounds
Laura Pappano

Something in Common

The Common Core Standards and the Next Chapter in American Education

Robert Rothman

Harvard Education Press
Cambridge, Massachusetts

Library of Congress Control Number 2011928649

Paperback ISBN 978-1-61250-107-9
Library Edition ISBN 978-1-61250-108-6

Published by Harvard Education Press,
an imprint of the Harvard Education Publishing Group

Harvard Education Press
8 Story Street
Cambridge, MA 02138

Cover Design: Sarah Henderson

The typefaces used in this book are ITC Legacy Serif and ITC Legacy Sans.

CONTENTS

ACKNOWLEDGMENTS

For the past two years, I have had the privilege of working for the Alliance for Excellent Education, which has played a key role in the Common Core State Standards Initiative. I have played a small part in that effort, which has introduced me to many of the individuals and events mentioned in this book. The book, however, was written apart from my official duties at the Alliance.

Nevertheless, the Alliance staff, particularly Bob Wise, Maria Ferguson, and Elizabeth Schneider, have been extremely supportive of my effort and generous in their ideas and advice. I am grateful for their support and proud to be their colleague. They and the rest of the Alliance meet high standards every day.

I am also grateful to the leaders of the initiative, who took the time to share their recollections candidly. Thank you to Governor James B. Hunt, Jr., Judith Rizzo, Dane Linn, Stephanie Shipton, Carrie Heath Phillips, Chris Minnich, Chris Cross, Sally Hampton, David Coleman, and Jason Zimba. Stephanie Shipton also shared with me a draft of a paper on the initiative, written by Michael G. Watt, an education consultant in Tasmania, which provided me with details on state plans that informed chapter 6. Jo O'Brien of the Colorado Department of Education and Jeff Nellhaus, then of the Massachusetts Department of Education, shared their state plans for implementing standards. While all of these individuals provided insights into the Standards and their development, any interpretations and errors of fact are mine alone.

I also want to thank Rick Hess for giving me the shove to get this project started, and Harvard Education Press—Doug Clayton, Caroline Chauncey, and Nancy Walser—who were true champions. They made the idea of getting a book on this subject so urgent that I agreed to a ridiculous deadline.

Finally I want to thank my wife, Karla Winters, and my daughter, Cleo, for letting me spend many nights and weekends hunched over a computer to meet that deadline. It is to them, and especially to Cleo, in the middle of her educational journey, that I dedicate this book.

FOREWORD

We are constantly learning something new about the state of education in the United States. And while we have made great strides during the past several decades, the discoveries aren't always favorable. Our young people are not keeping pace with their international peers in math, science, and reading. Achievement gaps still persist, and college remediation rates are abysmal. What's more, parents and teachers are not being empowered with accurate expectations regarding what students should know and be able to do to be successful.

Today's economic climate demands innovative thinking, collaborative spirit, high expectations, and a willingness to learn from the past and move purposefully forward.

In this timely and important new book, *Something in Common*, Bob Rothman lays out the case for what I, as a former four-term governor, believe to be one of the most important reforms I've seen in my lifetime: common core academic standards that are clear, consistent, and rigorous, and will help our students truly succeed.

As so well documented in these pages, these standards are the product of the belief among governors and state school heads that they needed—and wanted—to join forces and commission the best minds in the fields of math and English language arts, resulting in what are a superb set of standards.

For decades, I have been engrossed in the standards movement, about which Rothman gives us important and precise details. There are three primary reasons why I, along with so many other state leaders, support what has become a significant, reenergized movement in this nation.

The first is equity. Long ago, we established an equitable education as a civil right for all Americans. Having been adopted by nearly every state, these new standards will ensure that a child's education is not largely determined by where he or she lives, rather than his or her abilities. We must close gaps in opportunity and achievement that obstruct the success of all young people. Doing so improves their lives, helps sustain our democracy, and strengthens our nation.

My second reason is economic. The economy of the world is sharply different today than it was when my last term concluded in 2001. No longer can we define the fundamentals of an education by the same criteria that existed a decade or more ago. Students are competing with their peers across oceans and continents, and in an increasingly transient society, it is critical that what they learn is consistent and relevant from state to state. This is especially important for the children of our military who move frequently in serving our nation.

I remember Paul O'Neill, then CEO of Alcoa, asking at the 1996 IBM Education Summit, "Why on Earth can't we insist on universal standards at least for nine-year-olds? Can't a nine-year-old multiply nine by nine and get the same answer in all fifty states?" In the fifty years since that meeting, and until the standards chronicled by Rothman were released, we have made embarrassingly little forward progress in this area. Now, we are poised to bring about what the business community has long recognized as essential reforms. And for business, it's about more than the bottom line. It's about recruiting graduates who can read with high degrees of comprehension, are active listeners, and can think critically.

The standards creation process is my third reason, and Rothman effectively outlines the ironclad process within. He accurately discusses the movement as an initiative that arose entirely from state leaders who, too, recognized the importance of equity and the economy. He details the work of experts in the field, masters of the best science available about learning, teaching, English language arts, and math. And he rightly asserts that the products that emerged from those groups were tested against standards from other nations to ensure they would meet the test of competitiveness and by other experts who could attest to their rigor, teachability, and importance.

Rothman makes important distinctions when it comes to federal involvement with the standards, clearly illustrating for readers that the initiative has always been a state-led effort, and that no federal money was used to develop the standards themselves. It is equally important to point out that these standards are not "federal standards," and they do not equate to a national curriculum. Simply, standards are the *statements of the knowledge and skills* that students need to master in order to be prepared for college and the work force. Curriculum is the *road map* that teachers use to help young people acquire and master those skills. Depending upon the individual needs and learning styles of their students, teachers then develop instructional strategies and techniques to navigate the road map.

These new standards have not been *imposed* on states; they have *emerged* from states, much as the United States did almost 225 years ago when the Constitution and Bill of Rights were adopted. While I am not asserting that these standards have that status or weight in our nation's history, they will quickly become the linchpin by which states move forward to improve educational outcomes for all children.

It is essential that this book be read and serve as a thoughtful retrospective for those serious about the carrying out the vital task of implementing these new state standards. If we are to improve the lives of children for generations to come and reassert America's world leadership, we must all share a common understanding of this important development in our nation's history. Rothman's contribution here is immense.

Governor James B. Hunt, Jr.,
North Carolina

INTRODUCTION

A New American Icon

In April 1939, transportation officials and educators from each of the forty-eight states met at Teachers College, Columbia University, to discuss an urgent problem. A recent study by Frank W. Cyr, a professor of rural education at Teachers College who had convened the meeting, found that state standards for school transportation varied widely and threatened students' safety.

In some states, Cyr had found, students traveled in buses; in others, like Wyoming, they went to school in covered wagons. Bus companies had to customize their products for different states, which had different specifications.

Over a week of meetings, the group came up with a set of common standards for school transportation, and these standards were quickly adopted; one state, Utah, adopted them even while the group's report was being edited. The standards covered the appropriate size of buses, requirements for safety features, and perhaps most significantly, the color. The group wanted buses that would be distinctive and noticeable, even in morning fog. The yellow school bus was born.

That iconic symbol of American education has certainly kept millions of children safe over the past seventy years. But it also did a lot more. Because of improvements in school transportation, school districts were able to consolidate and operate more efficiently. In 1939, there were 117,000 school districts in the United States; a decade later there were 83,000 and a decade after that there were 40,000. Today, there are fewer than 15,000.

Improved transportation also helped improve access to education for students in remote areas and made it easier for children with disabilities to attend regular schools. More controversially, buses have also helped desegregate racially separate schools.

In many ways, therefore, the standards Cyr and his colleagues set in 1939 transformed American education. In recognition of his achievement, he was honored with a luncheon in 1989, on the fiftieth anniversary of the landmark conference.

Two decades after that anniversary, another group of state officials convened to unveil another set of standards. The Common Core State Standards set expectations for student learning in English language arts and mathematics at each grade level. Like the school transportation standards, they were designed to address the problem that state standards varied widely and, in some cases, harmed children. They also were aimed at making it easier for test developers and curriculum designers to come up with better products, rather than having to address the needs of different states. Most importantly, they were intended to bring about improvements in education overall. A century after educators and policy makers fought to expand access to schools, the Common Core State Standards were designed to ensure that students who graduate from high school learn what they need to know and be able to do in order to be prepared for postsecondary success.

Also like the transportation standards, the Common Core State Standards were adopted quickly; by the end of 2010, six months after they were released, forty-three states and the District of Columbia—which collectively educate more than 85 percent of U.S. students—had adopted them as their state standards. These states are now in the process of developing new assessments, revising curricula, and revamping professional development to align with the new standards.

The rapid agreement to the document represents a substantial step for the United States. Nearly two decades ago, attempts to create standards in core subjects prompted fierce political battles and derailed national efforts to define what students should know and be able to do. While these arguments, along with others over states' rights, did not go away, the Common Core State Standards have been able to attain a degree of consensus that has eluded standards advocates for years.

To be sure, as even the most passionate supporters of the standards will acknowledge, standards themselves do not transform schools. The record of the past two decades in which states developed and adopted standards, only to see schools make modest improvements, is testament to the challenges ahead.

Yet there is a great deal of optimism about the Common Core State Standards and a belief that they will help produce a transformation in American education—just as the school transportation standards of 1939 helped transform American schooling. There is a widespread agreement that standards should be common across states, so that all students have the same expectations for what they should know and be able to do—and that these expectations should be at least as high as those that other nations have for their students. The experience of the past decade, in which each state set its own standards and developed its own tests, left Americans convinced that states on their own would lower expectations and create systems in which raising test scores, rather than improving learning, would be the goal of schooling. A new system, in which all states had common, high expectations for student learning, gained rapid approval.

Over the past two decades, I have been a close observer of the efforts in the United States to set standards for student performance. As a journalist and as a staff member for organizations that have been directly involved in the standards movement, I have seen first-hand how leaders at the district, state, and national levels have worked to make standards the centerpiece of school-reform efforts. I believed strongly that this was the right approach, but I have seen how these good intentions have been derailed.

Since 2009, I have worked for the Alliance for Excellent Education, which has played a key role in the current effort to set common standards. I have followed the developments closely and participated in meetings and discussions that have advanced the common standards work. Some of what I report here I observed firsthand; most comes from published sources.

Something in Common is my attempt to explain the Common Core State Standards to a broad audience. The standards have the potential to transform American education, but only a small number of people are aware of what they are or what they can do. This is the first book to lay out how they came about, what they say about what students should know and be able to do, and what the remaining challenges are. This book can become the definitive volume on the early stages of this major development in American education—both a guide for practitioners who are faced with challenge of implementing the standards and a reference for those who want to understand how they came about.

Something in Common provides a detailed look at the Common Core State Standards and their potential for transforming American education. It describes the standards development process, the states' adoption decisions, and early steps by states to implement the standards. It explains in depth the content of the standards and what they expect of students. And it shows how the assessment consortia plan to measure student performance against the standards.

Chapter 1 begins by describing the standards that were unveiled in June 2010. It looks at the context of the announcement, including the federal Race to the Top competition and the competition for assessments. It discusses the unique aspects of the standards— their content, the research behind them, and the goal of common standards across state lines. The chapter also examines the role of standards in education and the research on the impact of standards in classrooms and schools. It shows possible reasons previous standards have failed to lead to improvements, and how the Common Core State Standards can potentially avoid those problems.

Chapter 2 steps back and provides a recent historical context for the effort. It examines early efforts at national standards over the past two decades, beginning with the standards of the National Council of Teachers of Mathematics and subsequent subject-area standards, and the sometimes fierce "curriculum wars" that erupted over the documents. The chapter also looks at the development of state standards in the wake of the collapse of the federal efforts. It discusses the wide variations in state standards and the growing concern over these variations. And it shows how anxiety over international comparisons led to an increased interest in national standards.

Chapter 3 describes the process of developing the Common Core State Standards. It reports on the diverse coalition that came together to develop and push for the common standards and highlights the key organizations involved and their roles. The chapter describes in depth the steps the groups developing the standards took to write the documents, the research they consulted, and the efforts they made to reach out to key constituencies. It discusses the feedback process—including the backlash from the emerging Tea Party— and the changes made as a result of comments from the field.

Chapter 4 looks in depth at the standards themselves. It shows the key features of each set of standards and how they are distinguished from existing documents. It analyzes the research behind the standards and how it informed the product.

Chapter 5 covers the state adoption process and discusses the role of national organizations in supporting adoption and the way federal incentives—notably, the prospect of Race to the Top funds— influenced the process. The chapter also describes the arguments that ensued in key states, such as Massachusetts, where there was strong backing for existing state standards, and the way electoral politics crept into the standards debate there and elsewhere.

Chapter 6 looks in depth at the plans states have developed to implement the standards. It shows how they expect to communicate the standards to stakeholders, how they are revamping curricula and professional development, and how budget challenges are affecting their efforts. It also explains how national organizations are developing curriculum and other materials and revamping their work to align with the Common Core State Standards.

Chapter 7 looks at the assessment consortia and their plans for developing assessment systems to measure the Common Core State Standards. It describes how the consortia came together, their proposals, and their initial steps toward development. The chapter also discusses some of the technical challenges involved in bringing their plans to fruition. The plans call for new approaches, such as a heavy use of artificial intelligence for scoring, that go beyond the state of the art. The chapter shows how the consortia, separately and collectively, are attempting to deal with these challenges.

Chapter 8 concludes with a vision of the world that common standards could help create: one in which students perform complex projects that lead to high levels of learning and in which assessments measure this learning and provide comparable information across states. But it also issues cautions about what it will take to realize the vision. It examines the steps needed in light of the budget challenges states face and possible compromises that might have to be made.

A word about terminology. The Common Core State Standards are a singular product, and states had to adopt them in toto, although they could add to the standards. For that reason, I have referred to these Standards as a proper noun, using upper case. States that have adopted the standards might choose to refer to them as their own state standards, but they are the same as those developed commonly.

This book is by no means the end of the story. The story continues to be written and will be written and rewritten over the next few years. States will be putting in place their plans for implementing the Standards, and these will affect classroom practice and teachers' work for years to come. The assessments the two state consortia are developing are not scheduled to be in place until the 2014–2015 school year, and states might need to adjust their plans to deal with technical and fiscal realities. A few states might revisit their commitment to the Standards if opposition arises. (See appendix A for Web-based resources to follow developments over time.)

At the same time, the common standards movement is poised to advance even further. The National Research Council, an arm of the National Academy of Sciences, and Achieve, an organization led by governors and business leaders, are leading an effort to develop science standards, which are scheduled to be ready for adoption by states in 2012. Standards in other subject areas might also be on the horizon. And the standards in English language arts and mathematics could be revised if the states uncover evidence as they implement the Standards that suggests that a different configuration of knowledge and skills is essential for success in college and careers.

For now, though, the Common Core State Standards represent a major sea change in American education. Thomas Boysen, the former commissioner of education in Kentucky, who oversaw the implementation of a complete overhaul of that state's education system, described that state's standards-based reform as the "second greatest revolution" in education in the United States. The first, he said, began in the early part of the twentieth century to increase access to schools and provide a basic education to as many children as possible. Kentucky's reform, Boysen said, "has the intention of giving every child the right to succeed in school."[1]

The Common Core State Standards represent a third revolution. The Standards define success more precisely than the previous generation of standards did: success in college and careers. They are more than judgments about what students should know and be able to do; they are statements, based on research and international benchmarking, of the skills and knowledge necessary for postsecondary education and workforce training. And they spell out a clear and logical pathway toward those goals.

Moreover, the Standards define these expectations for every child in nearly all states. They are based on the proposition that the quality of a child's education should no longer depend on political boundaries within the country. All American students deserve the education these Standards lay out.

That is a lofty goal. But American education, despite the many complaints and critics it has attracted, has managed to achieve some remarkable goals over the past two hundred years. Before any other nation on earth, the United States provided virtually universal access to schools, first the early grades and then high school. The attainment of American students has risen dramatically over the past century. And many students are learning a lot more than their parents and grandparents ever did.

Now it's time to take the next step to see if schools and communities can fulfill an even bolder vision.

1

STANDARDS AND AMERICAN
EDUCATION

ON JUNE 2, 2010, a group of educators and public officials met at Peachtree Ridge High School in Suwanee, Georgia, to unveil something that no one in the United States had ever seen: a set of standards for English language arts and mathematics intended to be common for all states. These standards were meant to replace the standards states had developed on their own over the past two decades, and were designed to spell out the academic knowledge and skills all students need at each grade level to be ready for college and careers by the time they leave high school.

The event was rich with symbolism. Notably, it took place in Georgia, far from Washington, D.C., to signal that the standards were not a product of the federal government. Leaders of the effort were quick to remind listeners that the standards were a state-run effort, under the auspices of the National Governors Association and the Council of Chief State School Officers. The list of speakers at the event—Governor Sonny Purdue of Georgia (R), Governor Jack Markell of Delaware (D), State Superintendent Steve Paine of West Virginia, State Commissioner Eric Smith of Florida, and leaders of the two national teacher unions, with no representative of the federal government present—underscored this point.

Like most events of this kind, the gathering in Georgia included a healthy dose of high-toned rhetoric. Governor Markell, who appeared by satellite, set the tone:

> Strong schools are the surest path to our nation's long-term economic success. America's students are now competing with children around the globe for jobs and opportunities after graduation. We need to maintain a national focus to ensure our kids are ready to compete and ready to win. That's why our nation's governors committed to this effort to create a common set of high expectations for students across the country. The Common Core State Standards reflect what can come from cooperation to improve student achievement.[1]

Others noted that the release of the standards document was just the beginning of the process of educational improvement. "We are entering the most critical phase of the movement for Common Core State Standards," said Commissioner Smith. "It is now up to states to adopt the standards and carry on the hard work of the educators and community leaders that worked to develop them."[2]

What exactly did the group of educators and officials unveil in Suwanee? Let's consider what these standards are—and what they are not.

The Common Core State Standards differ in several significant respects from the standards that have been in place in states for years. First, they are aimed at college and career readiness. That is, they are designed to lay out the knowledge and skills students need in order to be prepared to enter first-year courses in colleges, without remediation, or to enter workplace-training programs for careers that offer competitive salaries. By contrast, consensus panels of educators and subject-matter experts who were focused only on what they thought students needed to know at each grade level had developed previous state standards. These may or may not have been validated by entry-level expectations in colleges and work-training programs.

Second, the Standards are internationally benchmarked. They are explicitly designed to compare with the expectations for students in high-performing nations, those that regularly outperform the United States in international comparisons of student achievement.

International studies have shown that many state standards fall short of those of other countries.[3]

Third, the Standards are intended to send clear signals to students, parents, and educators about what is most important to learn at each grade level. Many state standards have been criticized as vague laundry lists of topics that teachers cannot possibly cover in a year.

Fourth, the standards are intended to be *common* across states. In contrast to the current system, in which each state defines for itself what its students should learn, the Standards are from the outset intended to represent a consensus among states about the knowledge and skills all students, regardless of where they live, are expected to develop.

At the same time, the Standards have their limitations. First, they are limited to English language arts and mathematics. They do not address all the knowledge and skills students are expected to demonstrate to succeed after high school. The English language arts standards set goals for the literacy abilities in subjects like science and history, but they do not consider the science or history content students might need to develop. They are a core, but not a complete program.

Second, the Standards represent academic competencies. These competencies are critically important, but they do not represent all of the abilities students need in order to succeed in college and the workplace. Studies of higher education and entry-level jobs have found a range of habits of mind, such as collaboration with peers and strong work habits, as well as specific skills that are necessary for success in addition to academic abilities. Students who master the common core might not be ready for colleges and careers if they have not developed these abilities as well.

Third, the Standards are only a first step toward school improvement. Even the most passionate advocate of standards would agree that the statements of expectations are hollow without efforts to ensure that teachers are prepared to teach to the standards and that students receive the support they need to learn what the standards expect.

Nevertheless, despite these limitations, the Standards represent a significant step forward in American education. As we will see in chapter 2, the United States has been engaged in standards-setting and standards-based reform for more than two decades. Despite these efforts, student achievement remains below the levels many policy makers consider acceptable, and achievement gaps between groups of students remain large. Why do the Standards offer hope for greater improvements? What's different about this effort?

TOP DOWN AND BOTTOM UP

One big difference between the Common Core State Standards and the previous generation of standards is the context in which they were developed and disseminated. As the next chapter will show, the standards movement began in the late 1980s as a top-down effort, where national groups and the federal government generated standards that were expected to be adopted by states or to influence state standards. When that effort hit political roadblocks, each state developed its own standards, in a bottom-up fashion, with uneven results.

The Standards were, from the outset, designed to be neither top down nor bottom up. Rather, governors and chief state school officers from forty-eight states—all but Alaska and Texas—signed a highly unusual memorandum of agreement to work together to develop standards that would be common across states. The leaders of the effort were the heads of organizations representing state officials, and they worked hard throughout the yearlong process to work collectively, rather than individually. In that respect, the standards were both top down and bottom up.

The leaders also sought to keep the effort at least at arm's length from the federal government. Mindful of the political controversy that helped derail national standards in the 1990s, the Common Core leaders were determined to keep politics out of the process as much as possible. That desire was particularly important because of the heightened political polarization in Washington: if the standards were seen as the product of a particular political party, they would never achieve widespread support. Thus, the event to unveil the standards took place in Georgia, and no official from President Barack Obama's administration was featured.

Nevertheless, the Obama administration had embraced the effort soon after taking office. In a speech to governors in June 2009, U.S. Secretary of Education Arne Duncan applauded the effort, while noting that it was led by the states:

> It is especially important that this has started at the state level because some people will raise concerns that common standards across states will lead to federal over-reaching. I am very sensitive to that issue. As I said before, I was a local educator before I came to Washington. Education is a state and local issue. You pay 90 percent of the tab, and our job is to support leaders like you. So let's be clear: this effort is being led by governors and chief state schools officers. This is your work and this is your agenda. Federal law does not mandate national standards. It empowers states to decide what kids need to learn and how to measure it. But common sense also tells you that kids in big cities like Newark and San Francisco, or small towns like Tarboro, North Carolina, are no different from each other. Standards shouldn't change once you cross the Mississippi River or the Rocky Mountains. Kids competing for the same jobs should meet the same standards. So while this effort is being led at the state level, as it should be, it is absolutely a national challenge, which we must meet together or we will compromise our future.[4]

Duncan and the administration also dangled before states a large inducement to adopt the Standards. In its Race to the Top program, a $4.35 billion grant program established as part of the American Recovery and Reinvestment Act of 2009 (the stimulus package aimed at helping jump-start the economy after the Great Recession), the U.S. Department of Education required states that applied to make four "assurances": to strengthen standards and assessments, to improve data systems, to enhance teacher and school leader quality, and to turn around low-performing schools. Specifically, under standards, the department asked states to show evidence that they have adopted common standards that are internationally benchmarked and that prepare students for college and careers—and that they have done so by August 2, 2010. Such evidence could include a copy of the memorandum of agreement showing that the state is part of a standards consortium, a copy of the final standards, or documentation that the standards are internationally benchmarked and that they prepare students for college and careers. Thus, without specifically saying that states must adopt the Standards, the department gave a leg up to states that have done so.

The department's scoring system for the grant competition also tried to walk the fine line between requiring adoption of the Standards and strongly suggesting it. The department awarded forty points (of a total of five hundred) to applications from states that adopted common standards by August 2, 2010. While states could earn enough points to win the competition without adopting the standards, the provision was a strong endorsement.

This level of involvement provoked responses from both supporters and critics of the effort. To opponents of the administration, the support for the Standards represented federal intrusion into state decision making. For example, Robert Scott, commissioner of education in Texas, one of two states that did not sign on to the Common Core effort, called the federal inducement a form of coercion. Yet the provision proved to be a powerful incentive for states to adopt the Standards—or at least, to do so quickly. As we will see in chapter 5, state boards of education in several states moved up their meeting dates in order to vote to adopt the Standards before the Race to the Top deadline.

The extraordinary state collaboration, along with the strong push from the U.S. Department of Education, helps explain some of the enthusiasm of the participants at the Suwanee event in June 2010. They recognized that the nation was on the precipice of an unprecedented accomplishment: expectations for student achievement in English language arts and mathematics that would be common across states. The needs for the future, not which state a child happened to live in, would determine what that child would be expected to learn.

Yet the enthusiasm also reflected the fact that the standards that were unveiled in June 2010 had the potential to transform American schools in ways that previous sets of standards could not. In order to understand why, it is worth stepping back to consider what standards are and the role they play in education.

WHAT ARE STANDARDS?

The word *standard* refers to the flag that soldiers in the frontlines would hold to signal to the armies behind them where to go. In public policy, the term has had two meanings. On the one hand, standards refer to the specifications of a commodity—for example, what constitutes an ounce or how long is a foot. Using such standards, manufacturers could make *standardized* products—that is, products that fit parts from different suppliers—because they are all the same size and dimensions. The federal agency then known as the National Bureau of Standards (now the National Institute of Standards and Technology) was created in 1901 to regulate standards for industry and commerce.

Standards also represent high aspirations. Selective universities, for example, set stringent admission requirements, and if they admit students who do not meet those requirements, they are often accused of lowering standards. In this sense, standards are goals that not all students can meet, but rather aspirations that all can strive for.

In the 1980s, in the wake of the report, *A Nation at Risk*, which warned of a "rising tide of mediocrity," educators began to talk of standards as aspirations. Yet they also began to express the belief that high standards could apply to every student. Invoking the mantra "all children can learn," educators developed standards that they expected all students to meet. This represented a profound change in American education. In contrast to traditional practice, in which some students learned at high levels while most learned basic skills, the new standards were aimed at making sure that all students, regardless of their backgrounds or life aspirations, would have the same educational opportunities.

In part, this effort emerged from cognitive science research that showed that clear expectations are essential for improving learning.

By making clear what good performances are, schools can signal to students what they need to do to succeed. Students know the criteria of excellence and can evaluate their own work against it, just as master craftsmen measure their work against standards they learned as apprentices. At the same time, standards are equitable; they set the same expectations for all students and do not suggest that some students can learn what they need to succeed after high school, while others are relegated to lower expectations.[5]

In the late 1980s, educators and researchers began to consider the idea of standards as the foundation for education reform. The intellectual underpinning for this notion came in an influential article by Marshall S. Smith, then the dean of the graduate school of education at Stanford University, and Jennifer O'Day, a Stanford researcher. In their article, Smith and O'Day argued that previous reform efforts, like curriculum reforms or teacher professional development, were ineffective because they were fragmented and piecemeal and did not provide sufficient guidance to improve instruction. Instead, the authors argued for states to develop ambitious goals for students that spelled out the knowledge and skills all students should have, and to align all aspects of the system—curriculum materials, assessments, and professional development—around the goals. At the same time, they argued, schools should be free to restructure themselves to meet the goals in whatever ways they found appropriate for their students.[6]

Smith and O'Day did not refer to "standards" in their article; they used the term "curriculum frameworks." They had been inspired by California's efforts in the 1980s to develop such frameworks and use them as the centerpiece of a reform strategy. But what they suggested was the same as what we now call standards-based reform: to spell out the knowledge and skills all students should learn and build the major components of a state's education system around them.

Unlike most researchers, Smith had the opportunity to put his ideas into practice. In 1993, he was named undersecretary of education in the U.S. Department of Education, and he helped lead President Bill Clinton's education policy. As we will see in chapter 2, that administration aggressively pursued standards-based reform by creating incentives and providing resources to states to develop standards. By the end of the decade, virtually every state had developed standards and a related system of assessments and accountability.

THE EFFECTS OF STANDARDS

What were the effects of this drive toward standards? The results have been mixed. On the one hand, student achievement has risen for some students in some subjects since 1990, according to the National Assessment of Educational Progress (NAEP), a federally administered test of academic achievement in core subjects. In mathematics for nine- and thirteen-year-olds and in reading for nine-year-olds, test scores were substantially higher in 2008 than they were in 1990. And the biggest increases in test scores occurred between 1999 and 2004, when all states had developed standards.[7] On the other hand, scores did not improve in reading among thirteen-year-olds or in either subject among seventeen-year-olds.

However, this modest improvement might not have had anything to do with standards. A 2009 study by Grover (Russ) Whitehurst, the former director of the Institute of Education Sciences at the U.S. Department of Education, found almost no relationship between the quality of a state's standards and mathematics performance, as measured by NAEP. Whitehurst looked at the issue while the Common Core State Standards were under development to urge caution about the effort.

In his study, Whitehurst examined ratings on state standards issued by the Thomas B. Fordham Foundation, a conservative-leaning organization that has rated state standards for more than a decade, and the American Federation of Teachers (AFT), a teacher union that evaluated state standards in the 1990s. He compared those ratings to state mathematics performance on NAEP or its gains over time. Some states, like Massachusetts, had high-quality standards and scored high on NAEP. But other states, like New Jersey, scored high on NAEP despite relatively low-quality standards. Similarly, Arkansas and California showed similar gains in NAEP math scores, but the quality of their standards, according to Fordham and the AFT, was quite different.[8]

Whitehurst proposed several possible reasons for the lack of a relationship between the quality of standards and student achievement. Perhaps, he suggested, "standards are such a leaky bucket with respect to classroom instruction that any potential relationship dissipates before it can be manifest. Alternatively, the Fordham and AFT ratings may not have captured the qualities of state content standards that drive achievement. Or NAEP may be too blunt an instrument to detect the influence of the quality and rigor of standards."[9]

The last two possible reasons are speculative. But let's examine the first possible reason in more depth.

It's become a truism that standards alone cannot improve student learning. That is because standards must be implemented; they must be integrated into state, district, and classroom policy and practice in order to have an effect. A number of studies conducted during the 1990s showed clearly that the bucket carrying the standards between state policy makers and classroom teachers was indeed leaky.[10] How state officials, district officials, teacher leaders, and classroom teachers interpreted the standards varied widely, and thus the effect of the standards as a policy reform was muted.

James Spillane, a professor of learning and organizational change at the Northwestern University School of Education and Social Policy, characterized such "standards deviation" as akin to the game of telephone, in which the standards reform was whispered from state capitols to the classroom, only to create a muddled message at the end of the line.[11] In a detailed study of nine Michigan districts from 1992 to 1996, Spillane found that standards-based reform in that state was intended to lead to substantial changes in instructional practice. However, because of the miscommunications that occurred between the state and classrooms, teachers interpreted the standards in widely varied ways. Some saw them as substantial changes in practice and made corresponding adjustments to their instruction, while others viewed them in a relatively superficial way, making few changes. The result was little overall change in student achievement.

Spillane noted that there were several factors that affected how the standards policy was implemented. At the state level, for example, a political dispute between the governor and the state board of education over the state testing program (the governor wanted to make it more powerful; the department wanted to reduce its influence) resulted in a cut in staffing and responsibility for the state department of education, leaving it in a position where it was unable to do much to support implementation of the standards. Districts, for their part, varied widely in their interpretations. In a few districts, local officials recognized the standards as fundamental changes in instructional practice, while others saw them merely as changes in course content. These differing interpretations were further affected by the level of resources available at the district level; those with greater access to human resources and strong professional networks were better able to spend the time and effort to help change instructional practice. As a result, teachers in districts that provided them with opportunities to learn about the standards and their implications were more likely than others to change their practices in ways the standards intended. They were able to improve student achievement, while the teachers that made more superficial changes did not.

Another factor that affected the way teachers interpreted standards and the influence standards had on improving student achievement was state testing systems. Recall that in the theory of standards-based reform, as outlined by Smith and O'Day, standards were intended to be the centerpiece of state policy; assessments, curriculum, and professional development were expected to be aligned to the standards to provide a coherent instructional guidance system. If any part of the system was out of alignment, the message would be mixed.

Assessments are particularly important. Researchers have found that teachers pay more attention to assessments than to standards, especially when the stakes attached to the tests are high.[12] Under accountability systems that states put in place in the 1990s and 2000s, the stakes attached to tests were indeed high: mandating sanctions for failing schools and, in half the states, requiring students to pass tests in order to graduate from high school. However,

in many cases, the state tests were not aligned to the corresponding state standards, and so if teachers focused on what was on the
tests, they were not addressing all of the standards. The mismatch
occurred despite the fact that federal law required that state assessments "must be aligned with the state's challenging content and
performance standards." And indeed, states commissioned studies
to show that the content on the tests matched that of the state standards. Yet independent alignment studies done in the wake of the
federal requirements showed considerable mismatches, and most of
the mismatches were in the same direction: the tests tended to measure relatively low-level knowledge and skills, rather than the more
challenging content and skills called for in the standards.[13]

Some of the misalignment was the result of the standards themselves. In some cases, the standards documents were vague, so that
almost any test question that measured a concept named in the standard might be considered aligned to it. For example, if a standard
required students to understand geometric properties, test questions that asked students about triangles, parallelograms, or line
segments could all be considered "aligned" to the standard, regardless of the depth of understanding they required. In other cases, a
standard might include multiple expectations—for example, asking
students to identify, explain, and interpret a mathematical figure—
so that a test item that asked students simply to identify the figure
could be considered aligned to the standard, even though it did not
address the breadth of the expectations for students.

In other cases, though, state tests were simply not designed to
measure what the standards expected. Many state standards, for example, expected students to be able to solve complex problems and
communicate their understanding, often in writing, yet the state
tests relied on multiple-choice questions that are ill suited to cap-
ture those abilities. This was the case in Michigan, for example, the
state Spillane studied in his examination of the implementation of
standards; there, the state mathematics test was exclusively multiple
choice, emphasizing students' abilities to apply computational rules
to answer questions, rather than to come up with their own solutions to complex problems.

Because multiple-choice tests are cheaper and easier to develop and score than tests that measure complex problem solving and communication, they became popular, especially after the No Child Left Behind Act (NCLB) required states to implement tests in grades three through eight and once in high school. At least fifteen states adopted solely multiple-choice tests in reading and mathematics to satisfy NCLB mandates, and several states, including Kansas and Mississippi, dropped open-ended items from their tests after NCLB required states to add more tests to their batteries.[14] Thus, teachers relying on the tests, rather than the standards, to guide instruction did not employ the teaching strategies the standards expected; it's little wonder the standards had limited influence on student achievement.

MISSING PIECES

In addition to the lack of alignment between standards and tests, the influence of state standards has also been hampered by inadequate attention to other aspects of the standards-based reform system. In a 1999 report, the National Research Council, an arm of the National Academy of Sciences, noted that standards-based reform implied that, if states made standards explicit, put in place assessments aligned to the standards, and held schools accountable for the results, then students and educators would have clear expectations for student performance and the motivation to change practice to support higher levels of learning. However, the report pointed out, these assumptions might have been overoptimistic and failed to take into account the fact that many educators and schools lack the knowledge and resources necessary to improve instruction and learning, and many districts and states lack the means necessary to provide them with appropriate support. "In our view," the report concludes, "standards-based policies can affect student learning only if they are tied directly to efforts to build the capacity of teachers and administrators to improve instruction."[15]

Unfortunately, many standards-based reforms did not do enough to train local educators in how to teach to standards or provide them with the support to do so, and thus the effects of the standards were uneven. Schools that had highly skilled teachers and administrators were able to use standards to develop new instructional programs that produced higher levels of learning, and schools where educators lacked those abilities struggled.

As with assessments, part of the problem lay with the standards themselves. Standards were expected to provide clear guidance to teachers so that they could design curriculum and instructional programs to support student learning. But many of the state standards failed to provide appropriate guidance to teachers.

In some cases, states in the early years of the standards movement developed standards by grade spans (e.g., K–4, 5–8, 9–12) rather than grade by grade. This practice, which followed that of the national mathematics standards developed by the National Council of Teachers of Mathematics and the science standards developed by the National Research Council, was intended to respect local control and avoid dictating curriculum. But unless schools made concerted efforts to draw a clear pathway to the end of the grade span, many teachers would be left wondering what to do. What is a sixth-grade teacher to teach when the standard spells out what students should know and be able to do at the end of eighth grade?

In other cases, standards were too vague or general to provide sufficient guidance to teachers. Just as test makers could claim that almost any item that measured a concept named in a vague standard was aligned to the standard, so teachers could say that any form of instruction that seemed to match what a cryptic standard stated was aimed at helping students attain the standard.

To see the difference between a vague standard and one that provided better instructional guidance, consider the following two examples. Both are from Indiana, and both are fourth-grade writing standards. The first (box 1.1) is from a set of standards adopted in 1999. The second (box 1.2) is from standards issued a year later. In the interim, state officials submitted their standards to Achieve, an organization led by governors and business leaders to support high standards, to review, and to make recommendations for improvement.

BOX 1.1

STANDARD 6: WRITING APPLICATION

Write using a variety of forms. Use reference sources to locate information. Use varied word choices. Write for different purposes and audiences.

Students in grade 4 who meet the standard will be able to do the following:

- Write using a variety of forms including responses to literature, informational articles, and reports.

- Use references and resources to find information for a report or description. Include details to support the main ideas.

- Use varied word choices to make writing interesting.

- Write for different purposes.

- Write to a specific audience or person.

Source: Achieve, *Measuring Up: An Achieve Standards and Assessments Benchmarking Report for Indiana* (Washington, DC: Achieve, January 2000).

As these examples indicate, the vague standard provides little guidance to teachers about the kind of work students are expected to perform, while the second, more detailed standard helps teachers understand the kinds of classroom practices—like the use of varied writing genres—necessary to ensure that students can meet the standard.

Even if the standards are clear and specific, though, they do not provide all the guidance teachers might need or want. They state the knowledge and skills students should be able to demonstrate at the end of the year; they do not describe the course of study that students should pursue in order to get to that end point. Nor do they describe the materials that should be used to support students' learning. For these purposes, teachers need a curriculum.

Whitehurst found that an effective curriculum can be one of the most powerful reforms a state or district can exercise. Examining results from evaluations conducted by the federal Institute for Education Sciences in 2009, Whitehurst found that students using the

BOX 1.2

STANDARD 5: WRITING APPLICATIONS
(Different types of writing and their characteristics)

At grade 4, students are introduced to writing informational reports and written responses to literature. Students continue to write compositions that describe and explain familiar objects, events, and experiences. Student writing demonstrates a command of Standard English and the drafting, research, and organizational strategies outlined in Standard 4: Writing Process. Writing demonstrates an awareness of the audience (intended reader) and purpose for writing.

In addition to producing the different writing forms introduced in earlier grades, such as letters, grade 4 students use the writing strategies outline in Standard 4: Writing Process to:

- Write narratives (stories) that:
  □ Include ideas, observations, or memories of an event or experience.
  □ Provide a context to allow the reader to imagine the world of the event or experience.
  □ Use concrete sensory details.
- Write responses to literature that:
  □ Demonstrate an understanding of a literary work.
  □ Support judgments through references to both the text and prior knowledge.
- Write informational reports that:
  □ Ask a central question about an issue or situation.
  □ Include facts and details for focus.
  □ Use more than one source of information, including speakers, books, newspapers, media sources, and online information.
- Write summaries that contain the main ideas of the reading selection and the most significant details.
- Use varied word choices to make writing interesting.
- Write for different purposes (information, persuasion) and to a specific audience or person.

Source: Indiana Department of Education, http://www.indianastandardsresources.org/standard.asp?Subject=eng&Grade=4&Standard=5.

two most-effective mathematics curricula, Math Expressions and Saxon Math, vastly outperformed students using less-effective programs. The effects were even larger for a preschool reading program, DLM Early Childhood Express supplemented with Open Court. The effects on student achievement were far larger, Whitehurst found, than for reconstituting the teacher work force, charter schools, and content standards.[16]

Diana Senechal, a former teacher from New York City who was involved in developing the Common Core State Standards, explains the importance of curriculum:

> [W]hen teachers know what they are supposed to teach, they can put their energy into planning and conducting lessons and correcting student work. If teachers have to figure out what to teach, then there are many moving pieces at once and too much planning on the fly. Also, there is too much temptation to adjust the actual subject matter to the students—if they don't take to the lesson immediately, the teacher may get in the habit of scrambling for something they do like, instead of showing them how to persevere. With a common curriculum, the teacher has the authority to expect students to learn the material.[17]

Many high-performing nations provide specific guidance to teachers without dictating how to teach. These countries do not develop detailed recipes for classroom practice; rather, they are in many cases lean syllabi that outline core content and suggested assessments.[18]

However, states and districts in the United States undertaking standards-based reform did little to develop curriculum and instead left the job largely to individual schools and to commercial and nonprofit organizations, like those that developed the mathematics programs that Whitehurst studied. Typically, textbooks ended up as the default curriculum. But because textbooks are intended to be sold to as many states as possible, textbook publishers do not generally tailor their books to align with a particular state's standards; they try to align them to many state standards, and the result is a long list of "facts, names, dates, topics, and concepts," rather than a coherent means of organizing a course of study to lead students toward the standards they were expected to meet.[19]

Professional development could help teachers overcome the shortcomings in curriculum, but there too, the supply fell far short of the demand, and thus the potential of standards to transform practice was unrealized. Most teachers began their careers before states set standards and were not prepared for the expectation that all students would learn to high levels. Nor were they prepared to teach in the ways the standards intended. For example, many of the state mathematics standards, following the lead of the National Council of Teachers of Mathematics standards, placed a greater emphasis on problem solving and communications in mathematics. Many mathematics teachers had been prepared at a time when mathematics instruction focused largely on procedural knowledge or the ability to apply preset procedures to solve equations. Enabling teachers to succeed with the new standards would take professional development.

Some states recognized the need to provide training for teachers and developed programs to prepare them to teach to the new standards. California, for example, developed a highly regarded set of "subject matter projects," led by the University of California, that were designed to prepare practicing teachers to teach in the ways that state's standards expected. A study of the state's mathematics project found that students whose teachers completed the projects outperformed those whose teachers did not.[20] However, few states offered such an extensive array of professional development opportunities tied to the standards as California. A national survey of teachers by the U.S. Department of Education found that most felt unprepared to teach all of their students to the new state standards.[21]

Studies of standards-based reforms show that these missing pieces—clear standards, strong curriculum, and professional development—made a difference in whether standards produced the desired effect of improving student learning. For example, a study of seven districts that engaged in standards-based reforms found that, without explicit guidance to teachers and expectations for instructional practices, standards, assessments, and accountability were not sufficient to raise the level of student achievement.[22]

Thus, Whitehurst's finding that the quality of standards is not related to either the level of student achievement or gains in achievement, according to NAEP, is not surprising. But what makes the Common Core State Standards different? Why did the participants at the Suwanee event in June 2010 seem so optimistic?

There are several reasons why the Standards have far more transformative potential than previous efforts. First is the content of the Standards themselves. Unlike many state standards, which are voluminous lists of topics that teachers find difficult to teach in an academic year, the Standards were from the outset intended to be parsimonious, coherent statements of what students need to know and be able to do at each grade level—"fewer, higher, clearer" was the standards writers' mantra. There is some evidence that they did not reach the "fewer" goal, but many observers agree that the Standards are indeed clearer and provide useful guidance to teachers. Thus, they are more likely than previous standards to set the direction for classroom practice.

In addition, as we will see in chapter 4, the Standards set out a logical learning progression over time. In many state standards, there is little coherence from grade to grade; in some cases, the same topics are repeated year after year, with little expectation that students are learning more as they advance from grade to grade. The coherence in the Standards can help teachers work together to design lessons and programs that will lead to improved learning. At the same time, teachers in one grade will have a clearer idea of what students entering their classrooms will have learned the previous year. In that way, the Standards provide stronger guidance for instruction than many state standards.

A second reason for optimism is the fact that in August 2010, the U.S. Department of Education provided $330 million to two consortia of states to develop new assessments to measure the Standards. These assessments are expected to include a greater use of new formats, including performance tasks that will take place in classrooms over more than one class period, and thus are more likely than most state tests to measure the full range of the Standards. In that way, they will encourage teachers to address a broader range of abilities than conventional state tests do and could also encourage a greater use of classroom practices, like projects and research papers, that lead to higher levels of learning.

Moreover, several of the key standards writers are involved in the development of the consortia assessments. Thus, the assessments are more likely than current tests to reflect precisely what the Standards expect, and teachers who focus on the tests will be focusing on the content students are expected to learn. Because teachers focus more on assessments than standards, particularly when stakes are attached to test results, the close alignment of the new assessments and the Standards will help ensure that the Standards guide classroom practice.

The third factor that is likely to enhance the influence of the Standards is the fact that they are common across states. When each state developed its own standards, publishers of textbooks and curriculum materials could ignore them in hopes of selling to a national market. Thus, the materials teachers used bore little relation to the standards documents they were expected to follow. But now that nearly every state has adopted these Standards, publishers have every incentive to align their materials to them. Likewise, teacher preparation institutions and professional developers who offer training programs for teachers from different states will need to pay attention to the Standards in designing their courses. Thus, the Standards are more likely than previous efforts to shape teacher development and curricula.

These reasons offer promise that the Standards will influence classroom practice and improve student learning. Whether that promise can be realized depends on a host of factors—the fidelity of implementation, the quality of the assessments, and the ability of states and districts (and independent organizations) to prepare teachers to teach the Standards effectively. We will consider these issues in subsequent chapters. But first, it is important to take a step back and understand how the nation got to this point. Why did previous efforts to develop national standards falter, and how did the idea for common standards get revived?

2

EARLY EFFORTS TO FIND
COMMON GROUND

GEORGE H. W. BUSH pledged to become "the education president," and he decided to make good on that promise by convening an extraordinary meeting in September of his first year in office, 1989. In Charlottesville, Virginia, the home of the first education president, Thomas Jefferson, Bush brought together the nation's governors for only the third time in history; President Theodore Roosevelt had convened the governors to discuss conservation, and Franklin Roosevelt gathered the chief executives to look at the economy.

The meeting was unusual also because the president and the governors agreed to produce, for the first time, national goals for education. Although education is primarily a state and local concern, Bush and the governors agreed that it was also a national responsibility. They noted that global economic competition demanded a national response, and the chief executives agreed that national goals would raise national performance.

Bush announced the six national goals in his State of the Union message in January 1990, and the National Governors Association (NGA) adopted them the following month. The administration and the NGA soon formed a group of governors and administration officials, known as the National Education Goals Panel, to monitor progress toward them.

The goals were ambitious; some called them fanciful. They pledged that, by the year 2000:

1. Every child will enter school ready to learn.
2. The high school graduation rate will increase to at least 90 percent.
3. All children will leave grades four, eight, and twelve having demonstrated competency in challenging subject matter.
4. The United States will be first in the world in mathematics and science.
5. Every adult will be literate.
6. All schools will be safe and drug-free.

At one of the Goals Panel's earliest meetings, Bush administration officials and governors recognized that they were not in a position to determine the status of the third goal without defining what "challenging subject matter" meant or determining what "competency" was. For that, the nation would need standards and tests that measured progress against the standards.

Didn't the United States always have standards for student performance? In a way, yes. States have for decades defined the minimum number of courses all students need to complete in order to graduate from high school, such as requiring students to take three years of English and two years of mathematics. But these mandates do not specify what students should study in these courses. They do not define what students should know and be able to do each year. The content of courses is in effect determined by textbook publishers, which produce materials that define what should be taught over the course of a year in a particular subject, and by test companies, like the makers of the Stanford 9—a common test administered by districts before state tests were developed, which determines what students should have learned.

The United States does have a national test of sorts—the National Assessment of Educational Progress (NAEP), a federally funded assessment program operated by the U.S. Department of Education. Created in 1969, NAEP has been an extremely well-respected monitor of student performance in core subjects because it has a long history and is well regarded as a solid test. The assessment has been able to track student performance over time as well as provide snapshots of performance in a particular year.

NAEP, though, has several limitations that restrict its ability to serve as a national standard for what students should know and be able to do. First, the assessment is administered to a sample of students nationwide, not to every student. Each participant in the sample takes a portion of the overall test battery, and the results are aggregated to provide results for broad segments of the population, not for individual students or even schools. This "matrix-sample" design enables NAEP to test a much broader range of knowledge and skills than most state or district tests, which offer a limited number of items to reduce testing time, and it can use some open-ended formats, rather than rely solely on multiple-choice questions, as many state tests do.

For the first twenty years of its history, NAEP provided results for the nation as a whole and for regions of the country. (In 1988, Congress broadened the program to allow for state-by-state comparisons, and the 2001 No Child Left Behind Act [NCLB] made state participation mandatory. In 2002, NAEP created a pilot district-level assessment, with six large urban districts participating. In 2011, twenty-one districts are participating in the Trial Urban District Assessment [TUDA].)

NAEP's matrix-sample design also creates its second limitation: it is a low-stakes test. Because there are no results for individual students or schools, there are no consequences riding on the results, and no classroom or school has a strong incentive to alter its program to improve performance on NAEP. By contrast, when a school's reputation or future existence depends on higher test performance, schools make great efforts to align their program with a test, sometimes in detrimental ways, such as inappropriate test preparation or even outright cheating. The low-stakes nature of NAEP is a strength; NAEP results are not the result of undue teaching to the test and thus are considered more reliable than other measures. But the test does not serve as the kind of guide for instruction that advocates of standards might want or for the kind of accountability for student learning that the Bush administration and governors were seeking in 1990 and 1991.

By the time the National Education Goals Panel had convened, however, the idea that national standards could help define what all students should know and be able to do had already taken root. In 1986, the National Council of Teachers of Mathematics (NCTM), the professional association of mathematics teachers based in Reston, Virginia, just outside Washington, D.C., named a twenty-six-member panel to craft "a coherent vision of what it means to be mathematically literate in a world that relies on calculators and computers to carry out mathematical procedures, and in a world where mathematics is rapidly growing and is extensively being applied in diverse fields."[1]

The mathematics council's report, *Curriculum and Assessment Standards for School Mathematics*, was released in March 1989, six months before the Charlottesville summit. The document was noteworthy for two reasons. First, it was intended to represent a consensus view of what should be taught in school mathematics to every student in every school in the United States. The standards specified the knowledge and skills students should know and be able to do, as well as measures for schools to evaluate their own programs.

The standards were intended to be a gauge for school mathematics programs, not a curriculum. In fact, the document organized the standards by "grade span"—e.g., K–2, 3–5, 6–8, or 9–12—rather than grade by grade, so that schools could shape their curricula any way they chose. For example, at the end of grade eight, the standards stated that students should be able to "understand, represent, and use numbers in a variety of equivalent forms (integer, fraction, decimal, percent, exponential, and scientific notation) in real-world and mathematical problem situations."[2]

The NCTM standards were also significant because in many ways they represented a sharp departure from conventional mathematics programs in use at the time. They placed a greater emphasis on the ability of students to solve problems and demonstrate their understanding of mathematics, and less emphasis on the ability to plug numbers into calculations and use formulas. They also recommended the use of calculators and computers as aids to problem solving. These recommendations would ultimately prove controversial, throwing the idea of national standards into question.

Nevertheless, the NCTM standards proved enormously influential, at least initially, both in schools and with other subject-matter organizations representing English, science, and social studies teachers. By one estimate, the NCTM standards were used as a model by forty states in revising curricula and helped inform the redesign of tests, such as NAEP.[3] The document also helped inspire other subject-matter organizations to consider the knowledge and skills that were essential in their disciplines.

The idea of national standards—and national tests—developed increasing support from a wide range of quarters. An informal advisory panel appointed by President Bush, separate from the Goals Panel and led by Paul O'Neill, the former chairman of Alcoa, began considering the idea of creating a national test that would be voluntary for schools. In April 1991, after receiving a report from the panel, Bush proposed an education plan, known as "America 2000," that called for "world-class standards" in five core subjects—English, mathematics, science, history, and geography—and a set of voluntary tests, called American Achievement Tests, to measure performance against the standards. When he announced his plan, Bush said he wanted the first test, for fourth graders, in place by 1993.

At around the same time, Saul Cooperman, the state commissioner of education in New Jersey, called for a federally funded test for twelfth graders. The National Center on Education and the Economy, a private organization based in Rochester, New York, teamed up with the Learning Research and Development Center at the University of Pittsburgh in a privately funded effort to create a national examination system based on national standards they would create. Calling their effort the New Standards Project, the groups enlisted seventeen states and six school districts to develop and try out the new system.

NAEP's governing board also moved to set national standards. The 1988 legislation that expanded NAEP to the state level also established a twenty-three-member quasi-independent board to oversee the program and authorized the board to set "achievement goals." Using that provision, the board set out to determine not only how students performed, as NAEP traditionally had, but also whether they were performing at the "basic," "proficient," or "advanced" levels. As Chester E. Finn Jr., a former assistant U.S. secretary of education in the Reagan administration and the chair of the NAEP board put it, these standards, which became known as achievement levels, would indicate "how good is good enough."

To set the achievement levels, the NAEP board used a process similar to one commonly used to set passing scores on tests, such as teacher-licensing examinations. But a trio of measurement experts the board had hired to evaluate the achievement level-setting process concluded that it was seriously flawed, in part because of a lack of agreement among participants on what constituted "proficiency"; the board dismissed the evaluators before they submitted their report. Subsequent reviewers also found fault with the process. Nevertheless, the board went ahead with the standards and used them to report results from the 1992 mathematics assessment. The board has since refined the process, and the achievement levels have been used ever since and are widely accepted.

One of the most forceful advocates of national standards and tests was Governor Roy Romer of Colorado, the chairman of the National Education Goals Panel. Although little known outside Colorado at the time of the Charlottesville summit, Romer became a fervent believer in standards and tests and was on the road constantly at education meetings in the early 1990s, usually brandishing a well-thumbed copy of the NCTM *Standards* and holding them up as a model for other organizations. In his talks, Romer often invoked his experience as a pilot to argue for standards and new assessments. "Nobody would fly with an above-average pilot," he would say. Rather, he would add, pilots are expected to meet clear standards—like the ability to land a plane with the engine off—and are assessed by their performance, not by a multiple-choice test.

With Romer's leadership, the National Education Goals Panel moved ahead to explore national standards and assessments as a way to determine whether students were progressing toward the third goal—"All children will leave grades four, eight, and twelve having demonstrated competency in challenging subject matter." But some members of Congress sought to put the brakes on the fast-moving train. No member of Congress was invited to the Charlottesville summit, but some members, particularly those with close ties to the civil rights community, were wary of national standards and tests. Led by Representative Dale Kildee of Michigan, a former teacher, and Representative Major Owens of New York, these members of Congress expressed concern that tests had historically erected barriers to advancement for people of color; they did not want to see any new barriers erected. So in June 1991 Congress passed legislation creating a commission to study the "desirability and feasibility" of national standards and assessments before moving forward to developing them.

The commission, known as the National Council on Education Standards and Tests (with the unfortunate acronym "NCEST"), represented what one member, Chester E. Finn Jr., called a typical Washington "Noah's Ark" panel: it included two senators, two House members, two governors, the presidents of the two national teacher unions, superintendents, testing experts, and teachers. But unlike many Washington commissions, which are largely ceremonial and leave most of the hard work to their staffs, the standards council was engaged from the start. Many members attended most of the meetings and, in full view of C-Span cameras, wrestled with the thorny issues involved in determining whether standards and assessments were indeed desirable and feasible. For example, at one meeting, members heatedly debated a plan to fully fund Head Start and other education programs to ensure that all students, particularly those from disadvantaged backgrounds, were capable of meeting national standards.

The council released its report in January 1992 and issued a ringing endorsement of standards, stating that high standards and assessments tied to them can promote educational equity, preserve democracy and enhance the civic culture, and improve economic competitiveness. The panel stated:

In the absence of well-defined and demanding standards, education in the United States has gravitated toward *de facto* national minimum expectations. Except for students who are planning to attend selective four-year colleges, current education standards focus on low-level reading and arithmetic skills and on small amounts of factual material in other content areas. Consumers of education in this country have settled for far less than they should and for far less than their counterparts in other developed nations.[4]

The panel recommended standards for students and for schools and school systems. For students, the council proposed national *content standards*, like those of the NCTM, which would spell out the knowledge and skills all students must demonstrate; and *performance standards*, like NAEP's, which would indicate the level of performance each student should reach. For schools and school systems, the council recommended *school delivery standards* and *system performance standards*, which would specify the resources and supports necessary for students to reach the standards. In that way, students would not bear the full responsibility for meeting the content and performance standards. Unlike the student standards, however, school delivery standards should be set at the state level, the council proposed.

The council also noted that standards alone are insufficient, and that tests influence what is taught. However, the council stopped short of recommending a single national test to measure performance against the standards. Instead, the council proposed a voluntary "system of assessments" that would consist of multiple measures of performance, not a single test. The system would include both individual student assessments and large-scale samples, like NAEP. The assessments could eventually be used for high-stakes purposes, such as high school graduation or college entry, as well as for system accountability, the report concluded.

To oversee the development and implementation of the standards and assessments, the council proposed the creation of a national entity, called the National Education Standards and Assessment Council, which would work with the National Education Goals

Panel to certify the standards and criteria for assessments as "world class." This proposal proved hotly controversial, as we shall see.

But the debate unfolded even sooner than council members might have expected. On the day the council released its report, a separate group of fifty prominent educators and civil rights leaders, including Theodore R. Sizer of Brown University, James Comer of Yale University, Marian Wright Edelman of the Children's Defense Fund, and John Goodlad of the University of Washington—as well as two members of the standards council, Marshall S. Smith of Stanford University and Keith Geiger, the president of the National Education Association, who had signed the standards council's report without indicating any ambivalence—released a statement opposing national standards and tests. In their statement, the critics warned that the well-documented inequalities in resources between schools and districts could turn standards into a "cruel hoax." They urged policy makers to focus attention on improving children's opportunities to learn, not simply to measure their achievement. This idea would resonate among Democrats in Congress.

NATIONAL STANDARDS MOVE FORWARD

The Bush administration did not wait for the council's report to embrace the idea of national standards. The administration issued grants to subject-matter organizations and researchers to develop standards in a wide range of content areas, including history, English language arts, science, geography, foreign languages, the arts, and civics. The goal, according to Diane Ravitch, who was assistant U.S. secretary of education at the time and who led the effort, was to "encourage professional fields to shape a consensus about what students should know and be able to do. Eventually, the standards would make their own way into the schools (or not) by virtue of their quality, as the NCTM standards have, and not because of the coercive power of government to impose them."[5]

Despite Ravitch's optimism, politics intruded. The biggest flash point was over the standards for U.S. history. History is invariably a contentious topic, since it usually sparks debate over different perspectives in a diverse nation on the role of prominent individuals and events. These debates play out in many ways, such as the well-publicized votes over history textbooks in Texas, where various board members argue over the inclusion of topics like the state's relationship with Mexico. The standards, developed by the National Center for History in the Schools at the University of California, Los Angeles, were no exception. The day before the document was set to be released, Lynne V. Cheney (the wife of Secretary of Defense and later Vice President Dick Cheney), who as chairman of the National Endowment for the Humanities had sponsored the history standards project, took to the op-ed page of the *Wall Street Journal* to denounce it in scathing terms. In an article entitled "The End of History," Cheney lambasted the proposed standards for placing too little emphasis on historical figures like Robert E. Lee and the Wright brothers and too much emphasis on individuals like Harriet Tubman and events like McCarthyism. The implication was that the standards were a monument to political correctness, rather than an objective definition of what students should learn about the past.

Cheney's article was somewhat misleading, because the references she cited were in teaching examples that accompanied the standards, rather than the standards themselves. And the standards were subsequently revised, earning plaudits from Ravitch and others. Nevertheless, Cheney's criticism hit a nerve, and the U.S. Senate voted 99–1 to denounce them. Senator Slade Gorton of Washington, a Republican who introduced the resolution, which was nonbinding, said the document failed to respect the contributions of Western civilization. "This set of standards must be stopped, abolished, repudiated, repealed," he said.[6] Although the vote was nonbinding and thus did not carry the force of law, the Senate action took much of the wind out of the standards' sails.

The standards for English language arts also hit rough shoals. The U.S. Department of Education had issued a grant to the National Council of Teachers of English, the International Reading Association, and the University of Illinois to develop the standards, but in March 1994, the department discontinued funding the project before it was completed. Department officials contended that draft standards were vague and lacked a "conceptual framework," and thus did not "define what students should know and be able to do in the domains of language, literacy, and literature."[7] Although the organizations went ahead and produced their own set of standards, the controversy mitigated their influence.

The political battles over standards and tests also played out in the halls of Congress, in large part reflecting Ravitch's concern over "the coercive power of government" and its influence on what students should know and be able to do. As noted earlier, President Bush proposed his America 2000 plan that was intended to provide support to help the United States achieve the national education goals. As part of that plan, he called for "world-class" standards in core subjects and "American Achievement Tests." It was sent to Congress in April 1991.

The Democratic-led Congress was lukewarm about his plan, however, and amended it, taking out provisions calling for standards and tests. Democrats, echoing their concerns about the history of tests as gatekeepers that had blocked opportunities for children of color, balked at the effort. The legislation ultimately got caught up in debates about private-school vouchers and never came to a vote. Although he set in motion the national standards efforts, Bush left office without a plan to carry them through.

President Bill Clinton was more successful, but he suffered setbacks as well. Clinton proposed a modified version of the revised America 2000 plan, which he called the Goals 2000: Educate America Act, that was enacted in March 1994. That legislation codified the six national goals (and added two more, on professional development and parent involvement) and provided funds to states to set standards and create tests to measure progress against them. That legislation was the first to establish the idea of standards-based reform as the centerpiece of state and national education policy.

Goals 2000 also created an agency to oversee the development and implementation of standards. In its report, NCEST had recommended the creation of such an agency to certify standards. Although this certification process would have no force of law, it would represent a kind of "Good Housekeeping seal of approval." Goals 2000 authorized the creation of the National Education Standards and Improvement Council (NESIC). However, this provision came under fire from Republicans, who called the proposed council a "national school board." The following year, after Republicans took control of the House and Senate, Congress repealed the provision before members were even appointed.

The political battles over the history and English language arts standards, and over NESIC, led some observers to contend that national standards were dead. However, some of the national efforts had an impact on educational practice. As noted earlier, the NCTM standards influenced national tests and curriculum in forty states. And the science education standards, developed by the National Research Council, an arm of the National Academies, in 1995, have been widely accepted and have had an influence on curriculum materials and professional development across the country. Their effect on teaching practice and on student achievement has been less evident, at least so far.[8]

In addition, New Standards, the private organization created by the National Center on Education and the Economy and the Learning Research and Development Center at the University of Pittsburgh, also developed a widely praised set of national standards in English language arts, mathematics, and "applied learning." Several large school districts, including New York City and Pittsburgh, adopted these standards.

ACTION MOVES TO THE STATES

While the national debates raged, most of the standards-setting action took place at the state and local levels. States and districts continued to select curriculum materials and develop assessments, and states increasingly developed standards to guide those decisions in the 1990s.

California was a pioneer in this effort. Well before the NCTM *Standards* were released, California, under the leadership of Bill

Honig, the state superintendent of public instruction, published a series of "curriculum frameworks" in major subject areas. These frameworks were not exactly standards—they addressed what should be taught, rather than what students should learn—but they served the function of defining essential content. Honig used these documents quite deliberately to guide textbook selection and, in several high-profile cases, refused to adopt textbooks that did not match the frameworks. He also intended to build a test aligned with the frameworks as well, but this test was scuttled amid a political skirmish between Honig and the governor that eventually landed the superintendent in jail on conflict of interest charges involving a contract to an organization headed by Honig's wife.

Kentucky was also a pioneer in standards-based reform. In 1989, the state supreme court ruled the entire state system of education unconstitutional because it violated the constitutional guarantee of equal educational opportunity, and ordered the state legislature to come up with a new one. The revised system, known as the Kentucky Education Reform Act, established six goals for student learning and seventy-five "valued outcomes"—standards—that spell out what students should know and be able to do. The law also created a new assessment system to measure performance on the outcomes and held schools accountable for progress. Schools that increased the number of students performing at the "proficient" level would be eligible for rewards; those that declined could be subject to sanctions. This system, designed in large part by David Hornbeck, the former state superintendent of education in Maryland, became a template for other states and districts throughout the decade.

Other states moved rapidly to develop standards, and the federal government provided a big boost to the effort. The Goals 2000: Educate America Act provided grants to states to develop standards, and more than forty states received funding under the law and used the funds to convene groups of educators and interested citizens to begin crafting standards documents.

Perhaps more significantly, the 1994 reauthorization of the Elementary and Secondary Education Act (ESEA), known as the Improving America's Schools Act, firmly put the federal government behind standards-based reform. In previous years, the ESEA had been aimed primarily at assisting low-income students by providing resources for additional instruction and remediation aimed at helping poor children improve their basic skills. But the 1994 reauthorization created an entirely new structure. Under that law, states were required to develop challenging standards for student performance in at least mathematics and English language arts and assessments to measure that performance against the standards. Significantly, the standards were required to be the same for all students, regardless of whether students qualified for federal compensatory-education aid or not.

Although some states opted out of Goals 2000, all states took part in ESEA because of the significant federal funds attached to it and were responsible for meeting its requirements to develop standards and assessments. Some states were slower to put the systems in place than others, however, and the U.S. Department of Education issued numerous waivers to allow states to miss deadlines. Nevertheless, virtually all states moved forward in developing standards. In 1996, fifteen states had developed standards; by 2000, forty-nine states (all but Iowa) had done so.

In some cases, the state efforts provoked many of the battles that had taken place at the national level as well and sparked some heated "curriculum wars." In California, for example, after the first state-by-state results of the National Assessment of Educational Progress released in 1993, showed the state near the bottom in reading achievement, advocates for basic-skills instruction denounced the state's curriculum framework, which had placed an emphasis on reading literature and fought to have the standards rewritten to focus on phonics and other basic skills.

Mathematics was also hotly contested. Backers of traditional instruction fought with advocates of the approach in the original NCTM standards, which focused more on problem solving and conceptual understanding. In California, again, the issue was particularly heated. The state's standards commission, which drafted standards for approval by the state board of education, worked with researchers involved in the Third International Mathematics and Science Study (TIMSS), a cross-national study that tested students in fourth and eighth grades in forty countries in 1995, to write a document that they said reflected the practices in countries whose students performed well on this test. That document emphasized students' abilities to solve problems and understand mathematics concepts, rather than simply to apply procedures, and suggested adding additional material in algebra and geometry in elementary grades.

But more traditional educators, led by a statewide coalition of mathematicians and parents known as Mathematically Correct, objected to the draft standards and wanted to replace it with standards that reflected more emphasis on traditional skills like computation and a more traditional course sequence. Their supporters on the state board rewrote the standards, which were then adopted. In the end, the two sides moved toward a truce. The NCTM subsequently revised its standards in 2000 to include a greater emphasis on computational skills as well.

Science standards, while not mandated by federal law, were also adopted by states. In some cases, controversies over the issue of evolution broke out. In Kansas, notably, the state board of education in 1999 approved a set of science standards that omitted the word *evolution* entirely, provoking a national outcry. The National Academy of Sciences and the American Association for the Advancement of Science, organizations whose science standards formed the basis of the Kansas standards, revoked their copyright, disallowing the state from using its materials. In the 2000 election, five members of the state school board were voted out of office, and the new board in 2001 issued a new set of science standards that reinstated the concept.

The state standards also varied widely in a number of significant ways. The variation was most evident from the rankings of state standards awarded by national groups that analyzed and graded them. The American Federation of Teachers (AFT) and the Thomas B. Fordham Foundation conducted semi-regular studies of the standards to provide a snapshot of the current status and to show improvements—and backsliding—over time. The Council for Basic Education (CBE), a Washington, D.C.–based private organization that supported the teaching of liberal arts in schools, also issued ratings, and Achieve evaluated standards for states that chose to submit their documents for review to the organization.

The organizations' ratings themselves varied, in large part, because they used different criteria for evaluating the standards. The AFT focused on clarity and specificity, reflecting their view that teachers need to know exactly what the standards expect in order to plan lessons. The CBE, meanwhile, emphasized "rigor," measuring the state standards against a framework the organization devised. The Fordham Foundation asked one or two university-based and independent scholars to rate the standards in their field of expertise; most favored a traditional approach to the curriculum, such as an emphasis on phonics in English language arts. Achieve used a "benchmarking" approach, in which the organization compared standards to documents that were considered exemplary, such as California's English language arts standards and Japan's mathematics standards.

An *Education Week* review of the reports by the three organizations that rated all state standards found wide variations. More than half the states, the newspaper found, received marks in mathematics that varied by at least two letter grades across the three reports. In English language arts, nineteen states had such differences. The variations in the ratings created some confusion in states and, in at least one case, became an issue in a gubernatorial race. In New Jersey in 1997, the Democratic challenger cited low ratings of the state standards to criticize the incumbent, Christine Todd Whitman. She countered by citing the higher ratings from another organization.[9]

The ratings showed that state standards tended to improve over time. The AFT found that some state standards that were rated most highly in 1996 were at the average level in 2000.[10] The Fordham Foundation, the only organization that has continued to rate state standards through 2010, found some improvement over time, but still found that the standards overall merited a C in both English language arts and mathematics. However, the ratings varied widely; California, Indiana, and the District of Columbia earned an A in English language arts from Fordham in 2010, while Alaska, Delaware, Iowa,

Montana, and Nebraska earned an F. In mathematics, California, the District of Columbia, Florida, Indiana, and Washington State received A's (Washington State jumped from an F to an A between 2005 and 2010), while Kansas, Montana, Pennsylvania, Vermont, Wisconsin, and Wyoming received Fs.[11] The variations in state ratings also reflected the fact that state standards included different content, thus expecting students to learn different things.

LAST TRY FOR A NATIONAL TEST

While the standards work continued at the state level, President Clinton, at least, held out some residual hope for national standards. At a summit in 1996 convened by the National Governors Association and the IBM Corporation, Clinton stated his belief that "being promoted ought to mean more or less the same thing in Pasadena, California, that it does in Palisades, New York. In a global society, it ought to mean more or less the same thing."[12]

To carry out that idea, Clinton made a bid to create a national test. In his 1997 State of the Union Address, Clinton proposed creating tests in fourth-grade reading and eighth-grade mathematics that would be available nationally, but voluntary. The reading test would be based on NAEP, and the mathematics test would be based on the Third International Mathematics and Science Study. (U.S. eighth graders performed below the average of forty-one nations in that study; students from twenty nations outperformed U.S. students.) The idea, as Clinton explained, would be to measure students in any part of the country against national standards. "We must start with the elemental principle that there should be national standards of excellence in education," said in a February 5 speech at Augusta State University. "Algebra is the same in Georgia as it is in Utah."[13]

Although some educators and public officials expressed support for the plan, the voluntary national test quickly ran into a buzz saw of bipartisan opposition. Chester E. Finn Jr., the former assistant U.S. secretary of education who was then the president of the Thomas B. Fordham Foundation, predicted as much when he quipped that no one would like national testing because Republicans don't like "national" and Democrats don't like "testing."

Finn himself and his ally, Ravitch, warned that a test managed by the Department of Education would be subject to political manipulation, and they urged the Clinton administration to take politics out of the proposal by moving authority over the test to the National Assessment Governing Board, which oversees NAEP. Secretary of Education Richard Riley agreed to this move, but that failed to assuage most of the critics. Representative Bill Goodling, a Pennsylvania Republican who chaired the House Education and the Workforce Committee, led the opposition. A former school board member, Goodling charged that the national test would usurp local control over education, which he wanted to preserve. As an alternative, Goodling asked the National Research Council to study whether existing state and district tests could be placed on the same scale to provide comparable results without creating a new test. The council's report concluded that the tests were too different to be compared in that way, so Goodling stepped up his opposition to the national test.[14]

Democrats, meanwhile, expressed concern that a national test could be used unfairly against members of minority groups, who traditionally scored poorly on standardized tests. They too asked the National Research Council for a study to examine the appropriate use of tests. That study concluded that tests alone should not be used to make high-stakes decisions about individuals, such as promotion or graduation.[15]

The opposition proved too much. Congress in 1998 agreed to allow the National Assessment Governing Board and its contractors to continue development of the test, but prohibited field-testing or pilot testing of test items. The plan eventually withered away.

NO CHILD LEFT BEHIND AND STATE TESTS

Standards and testing at the state level, meanwhile, continued apace. And once again, this activity was spurred by incentives and support from the federal government.

Shortly after taking office in 2001, President George W. Bush proposed No Child Left Behind (NCLB), his plan for reauthorizing the Elementary and Secondary Education Act. Unlike some members of his party, who wanted to reduce federal involvement in education, Bush proposed a strong federal role. He also modeled his plan in part on the system he oversaw in Texas, which had produced results that some called the "Texas miracle," despite some evidence that the "miracle" was overstated and masked high dropout rates.

NCLB, which Bush signed at an Ohio school in January 2002, built on the standards-based system established by the 1994 Improving America's Schools Act (IASA). But NCLB's emphasis on tests and test results was much stronger than the earlier law's. While IASA required testing in at least three grades, NCLB required states to institute tests in every grade, from third grade through eighth grade, and once in high school. And the consequences placed on test results were much more severe. Under the law, all states were required to set a definition of *proficiency* based on reading and mathematics test scores and set a goal that all students would be proficient by 2014, the year that students who entered school when the law was signed would graduate from high school. States would also set annual targets toward that goal, both for schools as a whole and for groups of students within schools (such as African Americans, students with disabilities, and English language learners), and all groups would have to meet the targets in order for a school to make adequate yearly progress (AYP). Schools that failed to make AYP for two consecutive years would be subject to sanctions, which would intensify over time if schools continued to fall below the bar.

In the years following its passage, NCLB was the subject of a good deal of vilification, particularly from teachers, and was blamed for all types of ills, often unfairly. (For example, some parents charged that NCLB was the cause of an epidemic of head lice, because principals insisted that students attend school even if they were infested with lice, in order to prepare for tests and take them.) Yet NCLB did have a strong impact on the emerging drive for common standards. Several provisions of the law, and the ways in which they were implemented, helped fuel that drive.

First, the law's requirement that each state set its own definition of proficiency quickly made clear that the word *proficiency* lacked a common meaning and that states varied widely in what they expected of students. This problem was particularly evident because of another provision of the law: the requirement that each state participate in the National Assessment of Educational Progress (NAEP). The results showed wide discrepancies between the proportion of students who were proficient on state tests, compared with the proportion of students who were proficient on NAEP. In some cases, the discrepancies were quite stark: in Tennessee, for example, 87 percent of fourth graders were proficient on the state test in mathematics in 2005, compared with 28 percent who were proficient on NAEP. In Massachusetts, on the other hand, 40 percent of fourth graders were proficient on the state test in mathematics in 2005, compared with 41 percent on NAEP.

There are many reasons why the results might be discrepant. State tests and NAEP do not always test the same content, so schools should be expected to focus on the material on state tests, which are intended to match state standards (although, as we saw in chapter 1, that is not always the case). NAEP has no consequences attached to the results, whereas significant consequences were attached to state test results under NCLB. Therefore, schools had much more incentive to focus on the state tests, and students likely did better on the tests.

In addition, there is no inherent definition of *proficiency*. That level is essentially a judgment, and judgments can differ depending on who is making them. Each state and NAEP set the proficiency target in basically the same way: they assembled panels of educators and laypeople and asked them to examine the test and determine the level of performance a hypothetical "proficient" student would attain and set a "cut score" at that point. It is reasonable to assume that some state judges might come up with a different definition of proficiency than the NAEP judges.

Nevertheless, there is evidence that some state definitions were set quite low, and that tests became easier over time as schools faced higher and higher targets to attain adequate yearly progress under NCLB. A study conducted for the Fordham Foundation by the

Northwest Evaluation Association (NWEA), a testing firm based in Oregon, measured state proficiency cut scores against performance on its Measures of Academic Progress (MAP), a test administered in schools in twenty-six states to supplement state tests. The study found that the cut scores ranged widely, from the sixty percentile (Colorado's third-grade mathematics test) to the seventy-seventh percentile (Massachusetts' fourth-grade mathematics test) on the NWEA scale. That is, third graders who were proficient in mathematics in Colorado scored better than all but 6 percent of students on the MAP but only the top fourth of students reached that level on Massachusetts' test.[16]

Moreover, the study found, in eight states, tests became easier over time, while tests were more difficult in four states, and improvements in passing rates could largely be explained by reductions in cut scores. That is, higher proportions of students attaining proficiency did not mean that students were learning more; rather, states were making it easier for students to reach that goal.

Did that mean that states deliberately gamed the system so that schools could meet AYP and avoid sanctions? Some critics said yes. In a report entitled "Hot Air: How States Inflate Their Education Progress Under NCLB," Kevin Carey of Education Sector created the "Pangloss Index," named for the character in Voltaire's *Candide* who continually believed that this was "the best of all possible worlds." The index identified states that presented overly optimistic reports of their own school progress. Carey wrote:

> The result [of NCLB rules and state reports] is a system of perverse incentives that rewards state education officials who misrepresent reality. Their performance looks better in the eyes of the public and they're able to avoid conflict with organized political interests. By contrast, officials who keep expectations high and report honest data have more hard choices to make and are penalized because their states look worse than others by comparison.[17]

Carey did not find a smoking gun. But even if his premise is incorrect and states did not deliberately manipulate their numbers, the variations within states made it obvious that some states expected higher performance from their students and schools than others. That meant that some states were not telling the truth: students were told that their work was proficient, when in another state it would not be good enough. Schools that were deemed acceptable in one state would have been targets for intervention in another. And the students who were affected by these variations were disproportionately students of color and English language learners, because the states with the lowest apparent proficiency levels tended to have relatively high proportions of students of color.[18]

Why should judgments about students and school performance depend on the state in which a student happened to live? That was the question that advocates of national standards began to ask.

Similarly, researchers also found that the content students were expected to know varied widely from state to state. A 2008 study by Andrew Porter and his colleagues at the University of Pennsylvania examined state content standards in mathematics and compared them with one another and with the NCTM standards. The study found very little commonality among the states, suggesting that there is no de facto national standard. Moreover, the study found, there was more similarity in different grades' standards within a state than there was between states. That is, a student was more likely to encounter the same content moving from, say, fourth grade to fifth grade in Arizona than she would if she moved from Arizona to California in the middle of fourth grade. As Porter put it at a meeting of the National Research Council, the repetition across grades sends the message: "Don't you dare learn this the first time we teach it; otherwise you'll be bored out of your skull in the subsequent grades."[19]

Porter's study pointed out a weakness in many state standards, especially in mathematics: they did not expect students to master a topic and move on to topics in a progression toward expertise. But it also raised the question that President Clinton had asked a decade before: why should algebra be different in Georgia than it is in Utah?

In addition to the questions about the content and performance standards, educators and policy makers also began to ask questions about the assessments that were put in place in the wake of NCLB.

Because of the law's requirements for tests in every grade from third to eighth and once in high school, a number of states scrapped ambitious testing programs that had been developed in the 1990s that would have been too expensive to maintain in every grade level. For example, Maryland had had in place a sophisticated test, known as the Maryland School Performance Assessment Program (MS-PAP), which asked students to work in groups to complete projects, among other tasks. In order to implement the program, the state employed a matrix sampling design, much like NAEP's, in which students in different schools completed different tasks; the results were combined to produce scores at the school and district levels, but not at the individual student level. But after NCLB became law, Maryland replaced MSPAP with a more conventional test that measured a narrower range of student abilities and produced individual student scores.

Connecticut tried to resist modifying its testing program by suing the U.S. Department of Education. The state argued that, although the federal government under NCLB provided $400 million a year to states to develop and implement tests required by the new law, these funds were not sufficient to enable that state to maintain its program. Connecticut asked the federal government to pay more to enable the state to add tests that were similar in quality to its existing tests, or else allow the state to continue testing in every other grade. The department, joined by civil rights groups, which maintained that the testing and accountability provisions of NCLB were essential to close achievement gaps, countered that the law required annual testing and that Connecticut could use state funds to maintain its program, if it chose to do so. A federal court upheld the department in 2010.

Other states, such as Mississippi and Kansas, sought to save money and produce results more quickly by dropping open-ended tasks and writing from their testing programs. Over all, fifteen states—educating 42 percent of U.S. students—used tests that were completely multiple choice in 2005–2006.[20]

Some states, however, were able to maintain challenging assessment programs under NCLB. Three small New England states, New

Hampshire, Rhode Island, and Vermont (later joined by Maine), formed the New England Common Assessment Program in 2002 in order to produce a common test, based on common standards. Officials in the three states agreed that, by joining forces, they could produce a better-quality test at less cost than any of the three states could do on their own.

That effort proved to be a harbinger of things to come. If those states could come together and agree on standards and develop a high-quality assessment to measure them, why couldn't all states do the same? For a number of reasons, the idea of common standards, which had effectively been shot down in the 1990s, would come roaring back again a decade later. And in large part, the impetus for the effort came from NCLB, which exposed the wide variations in state standards and tests. The notion of standards that would be the same across state lines, ones that would set high expectations for all students, gained widespread appeal and indeed came to fruition.

3

TOUCHING THE "THIRD RAIL"

A Common Core Takes Shape

IN JUNE 2006, former Governor James B. Hunt, Jr., of North Carolina pulled together a small group of education leaders in Raleigh, North Carolina, to begin considering an issue that only a decade before had seemed like a dead letter: national standards in education. The group seemed receptive to the idea. The notion of national standards, once considered the "third rail" of education policy—like the third rail on subways, touch it and you die—was no longer so dangerous.

To follow up on the issue, Hunt enlisted another former governor, Bob Wise of West Virginia, the president of the Alliance for Excellent Education, a Washington, D.C.-based policy and advocacy group, to continue the conversation in the nation's capital. In September 2006, Wise hosted a meeting in Washington on the topic, bringing together some of the leaders of national education policy organizations, such as the Aspen Institute, the Education Trust, and the Thomas B. Fordham Institute—groups that are active in developing education policy at the national level—to talk about whether to pursue the idea of developing national standards.

Although these meetings were held behind closed doors, they signaled that, less than ten years after President Clinton's proposal for voluntary national tests went down in flames, the concept of national standards had not perished in the ashes. What was different this time?

To participants in the discussions, there were several factors that made the idea more palatable—and pressing—than it had been in the 1990s. One, as described in chapter 2, was the evidence that state standards varied widely and that many states appeared to have set low expectations for students. The No Child Left Behind Act (NCLB), which required all states to participate in the National Assessment of Educational Progress (NAEP), had brought this issue to the fore. In some states, such as Tennessee and Georgia, the overwhelming majority of students attained the "proficient" level on state tests, but far fewer reached the proficient level on NAEP. But in other states, such as Massachusetts, the proportion of students at the proficient level on both exams was about the same. Clearly, there were discrepancies in what states expected of students.

Perhaps as a result, there were large gaps in student performance. A 2004 study by ACT, the Iowa City, Iowa–based organization that produces the widely used college-admissions test, attempted to quantify how large the gaps were. The study found that only 26 percent of high school graduates who had taken the ACT—students who indicated their intention to go to college—earned scores high enough to have a good chance of success in a college-level biology course, 40 percent were prepared for college-level algebra, and 68 percent were prepared for a college English composition course. The proportion of racial and ethnic minority students ready for college was far lower. And, the study found, because the expectations for the workplace are essentially the same as those for college, large numbers of students graduating high school were not prepared to enter the job market either.[1]

At the same time, there was a growing recognition that state boundaries were becoming increasingly irrelevant in an increasingly global economy. Thomas Friedman's widely influential book, *The World Is Flat*,[2] showed that the spread of fiber-optic cable made it possible for companies to outsource a wide range of tasks that had previously been performed within national borders, such as tax preparation and technical support for computers. Thus, U.S. students, no matter where they lived, were now competing in a global economic market with students from Shanghai, Bangalore, and Osaka. The idea that each state could set its own expectations for what students should know and be able to do seemed anachronistic.

Moreover, international assessments continued to show that U.S. students were performing well below the level of students in other countries. In 1999, eighth graders in fourteen nations outperformed those in the United States in mathematics and science on the Third International Mathematics and Science Study (TIMSS).[3] In 2003, U.S. fifteen-year-olds performed below the average of students in industrialized nations in mathematics literacy; students in twenty of the twenty-eight participating countries outperformed U.S. students on the Programme for International Student Assessment (PISA), a test administered by the Paris-based Organisation for Economic Cooperation and Development.[4]

The evidence from international studies showed that one of the key factors in the success of high-performing countries was the fact that they had a common benchmark for student performance. In other words, high-performing nations had national standards for students, rather than allowing regions or states within their borders to set expectations that varied widely.

The man now making the case for common standards, James Hunt, was persuasive. The longest-serving governor in North Carolina's history, Hunt had made his reputation in large part by enacting bold reforms in education. As governor, he created the Smart Start program, a widely praised effort to establish early childhood education and social services for young children. Hunt also served as the first chairman of the National Board for Professional Teaching Standards, which has set standards and awards certification for highly accomplished teachers since 1987, and he served as the chairman of the National Commission on Teaching and America's Future, which issued highly influential reports documenting the critical role of teaching quality in student success.

To Hunt, raising standards for student performance was essential to improving the economy, a subject he knew well in his postgubernatorial career as a lawyer. "My concern came from my involvement in the worldwide economy," he said. "I knew what was required with the workforce. On international assessments, we were not doing well enough—our students weren't learning enough. They were not as effective, as knowledgeable, as creative as they need to be in order for us to compete in the world economy."[5]

Hunt and his colleagues brought the idea of pursuing national—or, as he called them, American—standards to the board of his organization, the James B. Hunt, Jr. Institute for Educational Leadership and Policy, to see if the board would support the notion of leading a campaign for them. Board members, who included Diane Ravitch, the education historian; Kati Haycock, the director of the Education Trust, a Washington, D.C.–based policy organization that supports improved education for low-income students and students of color; and Governor Mitch Daniels of Indiana, encouraged the idea. Ravitch presented the board with a brief history of national education standards, and Daniels warned that the effort would have to be state-led, rather than run by the federal government. The institute agreed to take it on and start a campaign.

"It was very clear people did not want the federal government setting standards," Hunt said. "It would make so much more sense, it would be economical, and it would produce better standards if states worked together."[6]

As a first step, the institute commissioned the National Research Council (NRC) to hold two workshops on state standards. The NRC committee, chaired by Lorraine McDonnell, a professor of education at the University of California, Santa Barbara, commissioned papers that surveyed the views of policy makers in five states, analyzed the variability in content and performance standards and assessments across states, examined the quality of state standards and their effects on teaching and learning, and analyzed the costs of moving to common standards.[7] The committee concluded that the current system "is characterized by wide variation," and that it is not yielding the gains in student learning it was intended to produce. Specifically, the committee concluded, standards-based reform paid insufficient attention to teaching and provided too little guidance and support for educators. It noted that consistent standards may be a necessary tool for establishing equity, but that simply establishing them would not accomplish the goal and that there were numerous obstacles to establishing common standards. But the committee's report concluded with a call by Hunt to mobilize public support for common standards. The public has not been aware of the disparities in education in the United States, Hunt said, and of the urgency of eliminating those disparities. "I think this is so serious that the only analogy I can think of is World War II."[8]

Based on the NRC's findings, the Hunt Institute in June 2008 outlined a strategy for developing common standards. "If states are to develop a set of rigorous standards in common, guidance can be derived from the NRC's recent research and deliberations. If ever there were a time to build a better mousetrap, now is the time."[9]

The key components of a common state effort, the institute stated, are:

- "Define quality in content standards."
- "Establish an effective standards-development process."
- "Consider the influence of assessment."
- "Consider the influence of performance standards."[10]

Despite the seeming toxicity of the notion, the institute was actually pushing on a door that was at least slightly ajar. A number of prominent individuals and organizations had already been discussing the idea of national or common educational standards, and doing so out loud. For example, in 2005, the Center for American Progress issued a report pointing out the disparities in state standards and concluded, "Today, state testing results really tell the public little about how schools are performing and progressing. But the establishment and implementation of national standards and the testing and reporting of student achievement in two or three core subjects like reading, math, and science would provide the public with a much more accurate picture of how United States' students are progressing nationally and state-by-state."[11]

The same year, the *New York Times* published an article by Ravitch arguing for national standards, and *Education Week* held an online chat on the topic. In March 2006, Education Sector, a Washington-based policy organization, held a debate on national standards, and in September 2006, the Thomas B. Fordham Foundation issued a report outlining four scenarios for the creation of national standards. In recognition of the quixotic nature of the idea, the Fordham report was entitled "To Dream the Impossible Dream," the theme song from the musical, *Man of La Mancha*.

In its report, Fordham's Michael J. Petrilli, Liam Julian, and Chester E. Finn Jr. argued that national standards and tests were essential because state standards were inadequate to address issues like global competition and a fragmented educational marketplace, in which high-quality curriculum materials and teacher preparation programs were scarce. They suggested that national standards could be developed in one of four ways:

- "The Whole Enchilada," in which the federal government creates and enforces national standards and assessments
- "If You Build It, They Will Come," in which the federal government or a private organization creates voluntary standards and incentives for states to adopt them
- "Let's All Hold Hands," in which states band together to create common standards and tests
- "Sunshine and Shame," in which state standards and tests are more transparent, easier to compare to one another and to the National Assessment of Educational Progress (NAEP)[12]

The authors also weighed the strengths and weaknesses of the four approaches and asked a dozen education-policy experts to weigh in on the question as well.

Other voices also joined the chorus. Rudy Crew and Paul Vallas, two prominent urban superintendents, joined Michael Casserly, the executive director of the Council of Great City Schools, an association of superintendents and school board members from the largest urban school districts, to argue for national standards as a way of repairing "the patchwork system of U.S. that encourages high expectations in one community while discouraging those expectations in another."[13]

Federal lawmakers also joined the chorus. Senator Christopher J. Dodd (D-CT), and Representative Vernon Ehlers (R-MI) introduced legislation that would create incentives for states to adopt voluntary standards in mathematics and science that would be developed by the governing board of NAEP. Senator Edward M. Kennedy (D-MA) also introduced a bill that would encourage states to benchmark their standards and tests to NAEP; he stopped short of calling for national standards, however. And the Commission on No Child Left Behind, a bipartisan panel established by the Aspen Institute, a national policy organization based in Washington, D.C., recommended the development of model national voluntary content standards based on the NAEP framework and proposed that states could adopt these, build their own based on them, or maintain their own standards. However, if states chose the latter two options, the commission recommended, the U.S. Secretary of Education should issue regular reports comparing state standards to the voluntary national standards.

Despite the growing support for the concept, opposition remained at the top levels of government. U.S. Secretary of Education Margaret Spellings, who was one of the key architects and a major supporter of No Child Left Behind, cautioned that such a move went against "more than two centuries of American educational tradition," and suggested that local communities should set their own standards, rather than rely on "dictates from bureaucrats thousands of miles away."[14]

OUT OF MANY, ONE

While the rhetorical debate raged, a group of states quietly moved toward demonstrating that common standards were possible.

In 2001, Achieve, along with Education Trust and the Thomas B. Fordham Foundation, formed the American Diploma Project (ADP). The goal of the project was to make the high school diploma meaningful by aligning its requirements with the requirements for entry into higher education and the workforce. Such a diploma would signal to colleges and employers that students were prepared for postsecondary study. The concern was that too many students were graduating from high school unprepared for colleges and the workplace.

As a first step, the project surveyed college professors and businesses to determine the knowledge and skills students need to succeed after high school. Based on that research, the ADP defined a set of "benchmarks," or knowledge and skills in English and mathematics that students need to pass college-level courses and advance in workplace training programs.[15]

Using that research, the organizations leading the ADP formed a network of states that agreed to align their high school graduation requirements (coursework and tests) to the expectations of colleges and businesses. Based on the work in English language arts in twelve states and in mathematics in sixteen states, Achieve identified standards for college and career readiness in those two core subjects. A report of the work suggests that these states had come to agreement on a "common core of standards in English language arts and mathematics."[16]

The ADP went a step further. States in the network suggested that they wanted an assessment to determine whether students had met the mathematics benchmarks and asked the network to create a common algebra 2 exam. They chose that subject because few states had a test at that level and they reasoned that they could develop it more economically if they did so jointly. In 2005, nine states came together to develop specifications for the exam; six other states later joined the effort. (The exam would be administered in 2008.) Five states also joined to develop and administer an algebra 1 exam.

TOWARD THE COMMON CORE

Meanwhile, the organizations that Hunt and Wise first convened continued to meet throughout 2006 and 2007 to discuss the feasibility of common standards on a national level. The discussions dragged on for many months, as participants debated the roles the various organizations would play and who would take the lead.

Wise compared the deliberations to the Paris peace talks aimed at ending the Vietnam War, at which negotiators argued for months over the shape of the bargaining table.

Two additional organizations—the Council of Chief State School Officers (CCSSO) and the National Governors Association (NGA)—came to the table and made possible a solution. These two associations had been moving toward support for common standards. The NGA, under the leadership of Governor Janet Napolitano of Arizona (who would later become the U.S. Secretary of Homeland Security), had appointed a task force in 2007 to consider what it would take to create a "world-class" education system. Together with CCSSO and Achieve, the NGA examined the practices of nations that performed well on international assessments and issued a report that was intended to serve as road map toward that goal. The first recommendation: "Upgrade state standards by adopting a common core of internationally benchmarked standards in math and language arts for grades K–12 to ensure that students are equipped with the necessary knowledge and skills to be globally competitive."[17] That is, the organizations called for common standards that would be as high as those adopted in the highest-performing nations.

The state schools chiefs, meanwhile, grew increasingly interested in the idea of common standards after Gene Wilhoit came on board as executive director in November 2006. Wilhoit had previously been commissioner of education in Kentucky and had been an active participant in the American Diploma Project (ADP) network, and knew what could be accomplished if states worked together. He and his fellow commissioners and superintendents in the CCSSO agreed with the need for upgrading their state standards by adopting the idea of internationally benchmarked standards for college and career readiness, but they recognized that they lacked the resources to develop such standards on their own. By coming together and pooling their funds, they could attract the nation's best researchers and subject-matter experts and produce standards that were better than any state could develop by itself.

Mindful of the previous defeat of national standards in the 1990s, the organizations debating the standards effort—Achieve, the Alliance for Excellent Education, the CCSSO, the Hunt Institute, and the NGA—agreed that the project would only succeed if it was led by states; a national effort, especially one that carried the aroma of federal involvement, was doomed to failure. But as the ADP showed, states coming together to develop standards could succeed. Thus, the CCSSO and the NGA assumed leadership of the effort.

To gauge state support, governors' education policy advisers and chiefs convened at a meeting arranged by the NGA and CCSSO at the Chicago Airport Hilton in April 2009. The support was overwhelming. The state leaders agreed that variations in expectations for student performance were no longer acceptable, and that they should work together to develop common standards. "That was the moment I thought this might be possible," said Chris Minnich, senior membership director for the CCSSO.[18] The chiefs' group and the governors' association then drew up a memorandum of agreement, which would commit states to participate in the process of developing state standards. By signing the agreement, states would agree to take part in "a state-led process that will draw on evidence and lead to development and adoption of a common core of state standards (common core) in English language arts and mathematics for grades K–12." As part of the agreement, the states also committed to supporting the development of common assessments to measure progress toward the standards.

The agreement stipulated that the states would lead the process for developing the standards, under the direction of CCSSO and the NGA Center for Best Practices, the arm of the governors' association that conducts policy research and technical assistance for states. It also stated that the two organizations would appoint a validation committee to review and validate the standards, and that the process would lead to the development of end-of-high-school standards and K–12 standards in English language arts and mathematics. The standards development process was expected to be completed by December 2009.

The document noted that adoption of the standards would be voluntary for states, but that states that chose to adopt them or align their standards to them should do so within three years, or by 2012. It further noted that states could add additional standards beyond the common core. The common core would make up at least 85 percent of a state's standards in those subjects, however.

To indicate their commitment, governors and chief state school officers (and in some cases, state board of education chairmen) had to sign the memorandum. By June 2009, all but four states—Alaska, Missouri, South Carolina, and Texas—had signed it. In Missouri, Governor Jay Nixon signed the memorandum, but full agreement awaited the appointment of a new commissioner of education; when Chris Nicastro was appointed, she signed the agreement. In South Carolina, Governor Mark Sanford at first declined to sign the agreement, but then did so in August 2009. The governors of Alaska and Texas refused to participate. In all, forty-eight states agreed to take part in the venture.

From the outset, the NGA and CCSSO also took steps to formalize the project. In January 2009, the organizations held a forum in Washington to develop the Common Core State Standards Initiative. Achieve, the Alliance for Excellent Education, the James B. Hunt, Jr. Institute for Educational Leadership and Policy, the National Association of State Boards of Education, and the Business Roundtable were named as formal partners in the initiative.

At the urging of the Alliance, ACT and the College Board were brought to the table because of their extensive research in college and career readiness and to add higher education institutions to the coalition. The stage was set for common standards.

SOME SKEPTICISM

Despite the enthusiasm of the leaders of the effort, some educators expressed skepticism about the enterprise. In a number of forums, Jay P. Greene, the department head and twenty-first century chair in education reform at the University of Arkansas, warned that the effort could weaken state standards, rather than strengthen them. Greene suggested that a national effort to develop consensus could end up with the least common denominator. And, with the support of states behind it, this inferior product could be imposed on states that already had high standards. As he wrote on his widely read blog:

> Every decade or so we have to debate the desirability of adopting national standards for education. People tend to be in favor of them when they imagine that they are the ones writing the standards. But when everyone gets into the sausage-making that characterizes policy formulation, it generally becomes clear that no one is going to get what they want out of national standards. What's worse is that the resulting mess would be imposed on everyone. There'd be no more laboratory of the states, just uniform banality.[19]

Other critics, such as Sandra Stotsky, a state board of education member in Massachusetts who was influential in the development of that state's standards, went further and warned that the standards could enshrine educational trends. Rather than solicit research on what students need to learn, these critics contended, the standards writers might be susceptible to adopting educational fads. This possibility would be particularly harmful, the critics contended, because they would be imposed on most of the states. These critics were vocal, but did little to derail the effort.

PUTTING IT TOGETHER

The organizations leading the common-standards effort wanted to avoid the negative outcomes the critics warned about. They did not want the standards to be like the state standards developed in the 1990s, which varied widely in quality and effect on student learning. So they devised a process that would be different from the one most states had employed.

As noted in chapter 1, states tended to develop standards by bringing together a broad range of constituent groups, including subject-matter specialists, teachers, community leaders, and business representatives, who would try to come up with a consensus about what students should know and be able to do in core subjects.

The states would then send these drafts out for review to an even broader group and make changes based on those comments. The result in many cases was a long list of standards, too long to teach in a single year, that included all of the participants' pet topics, regardless of whether they were truly essential for all students to learn for later success in college or the workplace.

Leaders of the Common Core State Standards Initiative, by contrast, were interested in a leaner, more focused document that would support the goal of ensuring that students graduated from high school ready for colleges and careers. The leaders were especially influenced by a 2007 paper written by David Coleman, the founder of Student Achievement Partners, a New York City–based organization that assembles thinkers and researchers to design solutions to improve student achievement, and Jason Zimba, a professor of mathematics and physics at Bennington College. Coleman and Zimba, both brilliant, young Rhodes Scholars, had in 2000 formed an organization called the Grow Network, which produced innovative ways of reporting student achievement results. In their paper, which was written for Carnegie Corporation of New York and the Institute for Advanced Study in Princeton, New Jersey, they noted that their goal was to use student achievement data to help teachers improve standards-based instruction. But they were frustrated in their efforts, they noted, because of the standards that teachers were expected to teach. As they wrote, most state mathematics standards were "far too vast to effectively guide instruction and assessment across large school systems," and that science standards were also ripe for review. The title of their paper summarized their case: "Math and Science Standards that are Fewer, Clearer, Higher to Raise Achievement at All Levels."[20] "Fewer, clearer, and higher" became the mantra of the Common Core State Standards effort.

To begin the process, the organizations in the Common Core Initiative formed a brain trust, composed of representatives from Achieve, ACT, the College Board, the National Association of State Boards of Education, and the State Higher Education Executive Officers, to lay out a set of criteria the drafters should use in coming up with a set of standards that was indeed fewer, clearer, and higher.

Reflecting the impetus behind the initiative, the leaders identified as the primary criterion the idea that the standards should reflect the academic knowledge and skills all students need to be ready for college and careers. They defined college and career readiness as the ability to succeed in entry-level postsecondary classes without remediation.

A second criterion was that the standards must reflect research on college and career readiness. Topics that might be interesting but that were not shown to be essential for postsecondary success would be thrown out. The research did not need to be iron-clad; it should represent the best available knowledge. But, as we will see in chapter 4, this criterion served to guide the standards writers' work and minimized some of the ideological battles that had plagued standards setting in the past.

A third criterion was international benchmarking. The initiatives' leaders were motivated in part by the concern that the United States lagged behind its economic competitors in educational performance and wanted to ensure that the standards for student performance would be at least as high as those the highest-performing nations expected their students to reach.

To write the standards, the leaders of the initiative asked the three groups with the most experience and knowledge about college and career readiness—Achieve, ACT, and the College Board—to set up work groups in English language arts and mathematics and to nominate individuals from their staffs and consultants to serve on the work groups in each subject. Coleman and Zimba also were selected, in English language arts and mathematics, respectively. Others named included veterans of New Standards, the organization that had produced national standards and related assessments in the 1990s.

The initiative leaders also set up feedback groups to comment on the drafts produced by the work groups. These feedback groups included some of the nation's leading scholars in education, such as Robert L. Linn, the director of the National Center for Research on Evaluation, Standards, and Student Testing; Kenji Hakuta, a professor of education at Stanford University; and William Schmidt,

University Distinguished Professor of Education at Michigan State University and the lead researcher for TIMSS. The feedback groups also included some of the most prominent scholars in each subject area, such as Hyman Bass, a mathematics educator at the University of Michigan, and Catherine Snow, a literacy expert at the Harvard University Graduate School of Education.

In choosing writers, the groups consulted with officials from key states. The groups were looking ahead to what it would take to convince state officials to adopt the standards and wanted to be sure that states that already had well-regarded standards, in particular, would support the Common Core. So the CCSSO and NGA involved these states, notably California, Colorado, Florida, Georgia, Massachusetts, and Minnesota, in the process early on, first to suggest writers and then to review drafts.

The two work groups, in English language arts (ELA) and mathematics, were charged with coming up with standards for the end of high school—the expectations for students at the end of twelve years of schooling. These standards would signal readiness for college and careers and would guide the grade-by-grade standards that would be developed subsequently.

The groups worked intensively to amass research on college and career expectations and international standards. In face-to-face meetings, conference calls, and Google Group discussions, the groups hashed out the issues and shared and commented on drafts.

The NGA and CCSSO tried to shield the groups from the public eye so that they could do their work without getting bombarded with comments from the broader community. For example, they did not release the names of the people on the work groups and feedback groups until July 1, 2009, well after they started their work. The leaders of the initiative also planned to release the document after the work groups had ironed out most of their disagreements. But when the groups began sharing drafts with a small group of opinion leaders to gauge their views, one reviewer leaked the draft of the ELA standards to Robert Pondiscio, the communications director of the Core Knowledge Foundation and author of its blog, who posted it on his Web site. The NGA then released the draft officially, along with the draft mathematics standards, and issued with them a statement saying that the ELA draft had been "prematurely released."

Pondiscio's review of the draft ELA standards was scathing. Under the headline "Voluntary National Standards Dead on Arrival," Pondiscio wrote that the standards "offer almost no specific content and little that would be of use to teachers in planning lessons—or parents in understanding what their child is expected to know." E. D. Hirsch Jr., the founder of Core Knowledge, a Charlottesville, Virginia–based organization that produces curriculum materials and supports a network of schools dedicated to the idea that all students need a strong grounding in curricular content, added that the standards were similar to the "dysfunctional state standards already in place," which he said emphasize the skills of reading without specifying the content students are expected to read.[21]

The leaked document sparked a flurry of discussion in the education community. While some critics shared Pondiscio's and Hirsch's views of the standards, others were more positive. Alan Farstrup, the executive director of the International Reading Association, a professional association of reading teachers and scholars, said the draft "appeared headed in the right direction," while Henry S. Kepner Jr., the president of the National Council of Teachers of Mathematics, offered similar praise for the draft mathematics standards. Dane Linn, the director of the education division of the NGA's Center for Best Practices, cautioned that the organizations leading the initiative intended the drafts to go through several more rounds of review and revision.[22]

To be sure, the documents were revised. When the standards were formally released for public comment in September 2009 on the Web site set up for the initiative, they had changed considerably from the version that had been leaked two months earlier. The English language arts standards, for example, added several more texts illustrating the complexity of reading students were expected to be able to do, and the mathematics section added standards for mathematical practice in addition to the content standards. (For details of the standards, see chapter 4.)

The revisions did not go far enough to satisfy Pondiscio, who called the publicly released draft "vague [and] insubstantial." But the Thomas B. Fordham Institute offered a much more positive view. Reviewing the draft standards as it had reviewed state standards over the past twelve years, for content, rigor, and clarity, Fordham gave both the English language arts standards and the mathematics standards a solid B. For comparison, Fordham in the same study reviewed the frameworks for the National Assessment of Educational Progress (NAEP), the Trends in International Mathematics and Science Study (TIMSS), and the Programme for International Student Assessment (PISA). The NAEP reading and writing frameworks received Bs; the NAEP mathematics framework, a C; the TIMSS mathematics framework, an A; and the PISA mathematics and reading frameworks, Ds.

In their analysis of the Common Core English language arts draft, the Fordham reviewers noted that the writers had done a "praiseworthy job of defining essential competencies in reading, writing, speaking, and listening for success in both college and the workplace." However, they noted, the document does not provide enough content guidance for teachers. The mathematics standards, the reviewers wrote, cover "the essential content," but fail to set priorities among topics.[23]

The initiative also solicited public comment, and 988 individuals responded to an online survey about the draft standards over a one-month period. (Because the survey was online, it was possible that more than one individual submitted comments under a single name.) More than half the respondents identified themselves as educators; 29 percent, as content experts; 28 percent, as teachers; 22 percent, as parents; and 8 percent, as students.

Many of the comments focused on the standards initiative itself. Some commenters stated that standards did little to improve education, and some pointed out the need for curriculum and professional development to complement the standards. Some expressed concern about the level of transparency in the standards-writing process and said too few teachers were involved.

Regarding the English language arts standards themselves, respondents praised the standards and applauded the idea of "fewer, clearer, and higher" standards, yet many offered suggestions for additions without proposing what to leave out. Some of the most prevalent calls for additions were for standards for literature, rather than just for reading and writing, and a reading list that would define what all students should read.

Similarly, for the mathematics standards, commenters, particularly those who taught at the college level, proposed additional topics, such as exponential equations and analytic geometry. Those who taught at the high school level, on the other hand, questioned whether the draft standards represented a level too high for students who did not plan to go to college. They suggested some topics that could be removed, including completing the square, graphing linear equalities with two variables, solving equations with three variables, conditional probability, and modeling using probability and statistics.

GRADE BY GRADE

While the public comments were being submitted, the leaders of the initiative moved to the next phase of the project: developing the K–12 standards. These standards would provide guidance for schools about how to organize instruction so that students could meet the standards for college and career readiness at the end of high school.

This phase of the initiative called for a different type of expertise and approach than the first phase required. The institutional knowledge of Achieve, ACT, and the College Board was less important; rather, the need was for experts in instruction and cognition who could identify the progressions of student learning that would lead to mastery of the standards for college and career readiness. As a result, CCSSO and NGA enlisted a different and larger work team of fifty-one people in mathematics and fifty people in English language arts, although there was some overlap with the previous groups. The groups included individuals with expertise in assessment, curriculum design, cognitive development, child development, and English-language acquisition. Susan Pimentel, the cofounder of StandardsWork, a national organization that consults with states and districts on the development and implementation of standards, and David Coleman were the leads for English language arts; William McCallum, a professor of mathematics at the University of Arizona, Philip Daro of America's Choice (and former director of New Standards), and Jason Zimba were the leads for mathematics. (See appendix B for the full list of work team members and feedback groups.)

As they did with the college- and career-readiness standards, CCSSO and NGA also created feedback groups of experts to react to drafts produced by the work groups. The twenty-two member mathematics feedback group and the twelve-member ELA feedback group included leading scholars, business representatives, and classroom educators.

The CCSSO and NGA also created a validation committee to evaluate the final product and determine whether it reflected the research on college and career readiness and international expectations. The twenty-nine-member committee, chaired by David T. Conley, a professor of education at the University of Oregon, and Brian Gong, the executive director of the Center for Assessment, included a number of prominent education researchers from the United States and other countries, a superintendent of a large urban school district (Christopher Steinhauser from Long Beach, California), principals, and classroom teachers. (See appendix C.)

Like the first groups, the work groups for the K–12 standards met frequently in person, in conference calls, and in Google Groups, and shared drafts with officials in the key states. The groups had hoped to produce a draft for public comment by January 2010, but the date kept getting pushed back as they worked through their disagreements over issues like whether to include reading lists or whether to require mastery of the multiplication tables, and weighed the comments from state officials. Missing the deadline did not deter Kentucky from adopting the standards—it did so in February

2010, before the draft was even released—but leaders in other states grew nervous: they had to adopt the standards by August 2 in order to earn points for the Race to the Top competition, but the delays meant that they had a shorter and shorter amount of time to review the standards before the deadline.

The draft for public comment was released on March 10, and it received a great deal of attention. The *Washington Post*, which was given the exclusive right to publish the first article on it, ran an article on the front page. In it, the standards won praise from a wide range of quarters, including Democratic and Republican governors. There was also criticism from some groups, like the libertarian Cato Institute, which were known to be skeptical of the whole enterprise. Significantly, E. D. Hirsch Jr., who had sharply criticized the draft standards for college and career readiness, offered positive comments on the draft K–12 standards.[24]

Over the next few days, more and more news outlets covered the draft, and editorials weighed in. A *New York Times* editorial proclaimed "national school standards, at last," and concluded: "The new standards provide an excellent starting point for remaking public schooling in the United States."[25]

Public comment was overwhelming. Nearly ten thousand people responded to the online survey over a one-month period, and they registered a wide range of passionate views about the document. Nearly half of the respondents were K–12 teachers; 20 percent, parents; 6 percent, school administrators; 5 percent, postsecondary faculty or researchers; and 2 percent, students.

Overall, the reaction was positive—two-thirds of the commenters gave the standards high marks—but the comments also suggested some potent issues, both new and old, that the standards writers and the leaders of the initiative needed to pay attention to.

In particular, there were three groups of comments that expressed similar concerns. One group, which included comments from a number of people reflecting the views of the emerging Tea Party movement, expressed serious opposition to any sort of federal or national standards. Although the Common Core State Standards Initiative was state-run, this group of commenters objected to standards set by groups working outside their state and particularly objected to any involvement by the Obama administration. This is an issue that leaders of the effort have continually had to confront.

The second major concern was about early-childhood education. Although the standards started in kindergarten and did not address preschool, a large group of commenters expressed concern that the standards placed too heavy an emphasis on academic knowledge and skills in the early grades and did not match the early-learning standards for pre-K–3 that many states had adopted. Some early-childhood educators worried that the K–12 standards could lead to inappropriate testing of children in early grades or could be used as indicators of children's readiness for kindergarten.[26]

In a further expression of their concern, some four hundred early-childhood educators signed a statement, organized by the Alliance for Childhood, a College Park, Maryland–based organization that promotes policies for children, objecting to the draft Common Core State Standards. The statement argued that the standards conflicted with research on how children learn and how to teach in the early grades. It called on the NGA and CCSSO to withdraw the standards and instead called for the creation of a "consortium of early childhood researchers, developmental psychologists, pediatricians, cognitive scientists, master teachers, and school leaders to develop comprehensive guidelines for effective early care and teaching that recognize the right of every child to a healthy start in life and a developmentally appropriate education."[27]

A third group of comments on the draft Common Core State Standards also expressed concerns that the document focused too narrowly on academic knowledge and skills, rather than other outcomes for children and youth. This group called for health standards to accompany the content standards.

In addition to these general concerns, commenters also called for standards in other subjects like science and social studies, and expressed concern about assessment and the implementation of the standards.

The comments about the standards themselves were generally positive, but commenters also offered suggestions that the standards writers took seriously as they made revisions. For example, several people said that the standards for grade bands (e.g., 9–10, 11–12) in the English language arts standards were confusing and, as one commenter put it, would make "vertical alignment a nightmare." The final version maintained that organization.

GOOD TO GREAT

The review period provided an opportunity for standards writers to strengthen the document. By reviewing the comments from the public, soliciting opinions from experts who had not been consulted in the early stages, and going over their work, the writers were able to improve their draft substantially. As Zimba put it, the standards went from "good to great"—echoing a phrase made popular by Jim Collins, the author of a book by the same name—between March and June 2010, when they were released in final form to the public.

And, indeed, the final version won high marks from those who had followed its development closely. The Fordham Institute, which had awarded the draft standards for college and career readiness Bs in English language arts and mathematics, gave the final version a B+ in English and an A– in mathematics. Moreover, these grades were significantly higher than those Fordham had awarded to most state standards. The Common Core State Standards were superior to those in thirty-nine states in mathematics and thirty-seven states in English. In thirty-three states, the Standards were superior to the standards in both subjects, the Fordham review concluded. In only three jurisdictions were state standards superior to the Common Core, it found.[28]

Perhaps more significantly, the validation committee, the panel appointed by the NGA and CCSSO to assess whether the Common Core State Standards were consistent with the research on readiness for college and career readiness and other nations' standards, gave the document a strong vote of confidence. Specifically, the panel of researchers and practitioners concluded that the Standards were:

- "Reflective of the core knowledge and skills in ELA and mathematics that students need to be college- and career-ready"
- "Appropriate in terms of their level of clarity and specificity"
- "Comparable to the expectations of other leading nations"
- "Informed by available research or evidence"
- "The result of processes that reflect best practices for standards development"
- "A solid starting point for adoption of cross-state common core standards"
- "A sound basis for eventual development of standards-based assessments"[29]

These two reports helped bolster the case within states for adopting the Common Core State Standards. But the biggest selling point for the Standards was the document itself. As they hoped to do, the drafters of the Standards produced a set of expectations for student learning that spells out in clear terms what all students need to know and be able to do at each grade level, and focuses on the most important concepts and skills. The document indeed differs from many state standards and calls for substantial departures from conventional practice in many areas. Its recommendations deserve a close look.

4

GREAT EXPECTATIONS

How the Common Core Stands Apart

ON THE SURFACE, the Common Core State Standards unveiled in Suwanee, Georgia, on June 2, 2010, are similar to many of the standards states have developed over the past two decades. They are divided into two subject areas, English language arts and mathematics; they describe a discrete set of content knowledge and skills for each subject and a set of objectives within each standard; and they offer goals for each grade level, kindergarten through grade twelve.

Beneath the surface, though, the Common Core State Standards represent a substantial shift from many previous state standards. These shifts are evident in both how the document can be read and what the Standards expect students to know and be able to do. For those reasons, the Standards imply substantial changes in what teachers should do in the classroom and thus what they should know and be able to do to teach students to the Standards effectively; yet, at the same time, the Standards represent a useful and user-friendly guide to the kinds of changes that are necessary. They truly are a clear statement of what all students need to learn.

"FEWER, CLEARER, HIGHER"

To consider what the standards say and what they imply about classroom practice, it is worth looking first at the criteria the standards writers used to develop them. According to several participants in the process, the standards writers' adherence to these criteria helped them avoid some of the ideological wars that have plagued standards setting in the past and maintain a focus on those things considered necessary for students to learn to become successful adults.

The first criterion was the standards' mantra—"fewer, clearer, and higher," as David Coleman and Jason Zimba had proposed in their paper. By adhering to this criterion, the organizers believed, the standards would be more likely to drive effective policy and practice.

"Fewer" was an important goal. One of the most common criticisms of state standards was that they tended to be long lists of objectives, too many to teach in a single year and far too many for teachers and students to make sense of. In part, this problem resulted from the way many of the standards were developed. State agencies tended to bring together teachers and subject-matter experts, all of whom had strong opinions about what should be taught in a particular subject, and agencies determined that the best way they could get an agreement would be to accept all of their ideas. They then went to the community for input and got some more ideas to add to the mix.

By seeking more parsimony from the outset, the standards writers were forced to make hard decisions about what was most important and what they could leave out. They were guided by the goal of ensuring that the standards would be coherent and make sense to students, parents, and teachers, and that they could serve as an effective guide to practice.

In the end, the writers might have achieved only partial success toward the "fewer" goal. A study by Andrew Porter and his colleagues at the University of Pennsylvania found that, in mathematics, the Common Core State Standards included fewer topics than state standards in grades K through five; however, the Standards included more topics than the states in grades six through twelve. In

English language arts, the Common Core State Standards included more topics than the states at every grade level.[1]

But the standards writers counter that the number of topics are not the best way to measure the Standards. The ten "anchor" standards in English language arts are fewer than the large number of separate standards in many state documents, and the mathematics standards are grouped in fewer categories than many state standards.

"Clearer" was related to fewer: if the standards were coherent, teachers would more likely understand and use them. To that end, the standard writers attempted to use language that would be understandable, rather than vague generalities that could mean many things to many people. In addition, they relied on theories of learning that showed how students progress from a novice state toward mastery. We will see more about these "learning progressions" later in this chapter.

"Higher" was a critical goal, both to ensure that the Standards would be adopted and to ensure that they reflected the goal of preparing all students for colleges and careers. The variations in state standards that helped fuel the effort toward Common Core State Standards made clear that the expectations for students were too low in some states and that students who were considered proficient on state standards did not attain all the knowledge and skills they would need to succeed after high school. By raising standards in states that set them too low, the Common Core would make clear what is expected for college and career readiness. At the same time, the organizers of the effort wanted states that had set high standards to embrace them as well, so that they would truly be common across states. To achieve their support, the Common Core needed to be at least as high as the highest state standards. The standards writers used the state standards as important guidelines for their own work and could show that they built on the best of what states had done.

There is some evidence that the Common Core State Standards are indeed higher than existing standards. A study that compared the Common Core mathematics standards with publicly released items from the eighth-grade National Assessment of Educational Progress (NAEP) mathematics test found that the NAEP items were two to three years below the Common Core eighth-grade standards. That is, NAEP included content in its eighth-grade mathematics test that the Common Core State Standards expect students to learn in fifth or sixth grade.[2]

In addition to the criterion of "fewer, clearer, and higher," the standards writers also hewed to evidence about college and career readiness. They defined readiness as the ability to succeed in entry-level, credit-bearing, academic college courses and in workforce training programs. That is, students who met the standards should be able to enroll in postsecondary education without the need for remediation. For college, that meant enrolling in either a two-year or four-year institution; for workforce training, that meant enrolling in programs that prepare students for careers that offer competitive, livable salaries, that offer opportunities for career advancement, and that are in a growing or sustainable industry.

This criterion set clear parameters for the standards writers. They had to gather evidence about precisely what is necessary for college and careers and weigh each proposed standard against that evidence. They could then eliminate some topics that might be important but not essential and focus on topics that were most critical.

A third important criterion was international benchmarking. Recall that leaders of the standards effort were concerned that the changes in the global economy and society meant that U.S. students would be competing with peers from around the world, not just those across the street. That meant that American children would have to learn to the same level as their international counterparts, who continually outperformed U.S. students on cross-national tests.

To meet this criterion, the standards writers examined standards documents from high-performing nations like Finland and Singapore and made judgments about topics that those nations considered vital. They also looked at them to see when the important topics were taught and made sure that U.S. students would be on track to higher levels of learning at the end of high school.

TWO SETS OF STANDARDS

The Common Core State Standards are in two parts that were developed separately, but are embedded and linked together in the final document. The first is the set of standards for college and career readiness. These in effect represent the end point, the standards students would be expected to reach at the end of high school in order to be prepared to enter a college or workforce training program.

To develop the standards for college and career readiness, the standards writers started with evidence from postsecondary education and the workplace. For example, ACT has identified the knowledge and skills that students who attained the benchmark score (21 out of 36) on the reading portion of its college-admissions test. Students who attained that score had a high probability of earning a C or better in a first-year history or psychology course, and a 50 percent chance of earning a B or better.[3]

They also conducted their own research by buying introductory college textbooks and studying the kinds of reading and mathematics students would be expected to do in their first year in college. And they asked teachers of first-year college courses to confirm their judgments about what students should know and be able to do.

The standards for college and career readiness then became the anchor standards for the entire program. The standards writers developed a careful sequence, or "staircase," as they called it, of corresponding grade-level standards that would lead students to the standards for college and career readiness.

In doing so, the standards writers paid careful attention to *learning progressions*. In recent years, researchers and practitioners have outlined models that describe the knowledge and skills within a subject area and the sequence in which they typically develop over time. These learning progressions have served as the basis for assessments that can measure where students are on the continuum from novice to expert. For example, the Australian Council for Educational Research has developed "progress maps" to guide the creation of the Developmental Assessment program, which is used in several states in that country.[4]

The Common Core State Standards identified learning progressions to show how students develop in competency over time. In English language arts, for example, the Standards identify a basic set of language skills that should be mastered in the grade level in which they are introduced, but that need to be retaught in more sophisticated ways as students develop their reading and writing abilities. In third grade, the Standards state, students should learn subject-verb and pronoun-antecedent agreement; in fourth grade, they should learn to produce complete sentences; in fifth grade, students should recognize and correct inappropriate shifts in verb tense; in sixth grade, students should recognize and correct inappropriate shifts in pronoun number and person; in seventh grade, they should place phrases and clauses within a sentence, recognizing and correcting misplaced modifiers; in eighth grade, they should recognize and correct inappropriate shifts in verb choice and mood; and in ninth grade, they should use parallel structure.

In mathematics, there are a number of progressions toward deeper understanding of core concepts. For example, in third grade, students are expected to understand fractions as numbers. In fourth grade, students are expected to extend their understanding by demonstrating that they can add and subtract fractions. In fifth grade, students are expected to understand multiplication and division of fractions.

ENGLISH LANGUAGE ARTS STANDARDS

The chapter headings in the sixty-six-page Common Core English language arts standards show two major differences from most state standards. The first is the fact that there are standards for reading, writing, speaking, and listening. Most states have standards for the first two, but the last two are rare. But as the standards make clear, oral language is a vital mode of communication in college and the workplace. Students need to know how to be able to make presentations and to understand presentations by teachers and peers.

Moreover, oral language and written language are interdependent; in the early grades, students' comprehension of oral language helps them develop comprehension of written texts. As the document states:

> Oral language development precedes and is the foundation for written language development; in other words, oral language is primary and written language builds on it. For children in preschool and the early grades, receptive and expressive abilities do not develop simultaneously or at the same pace: receptive language generally precedes expressive language. Children need to be able to understand words before they can produce and use them.[5]

The second major difference between the Common Core State Standards and most state standards in English language arts is the inclusion of standards for "literacy in history/social studies, science, and technical subjects." The inclusion of these standards reflects research that shows clearly that the literacy demands of the content areas are unique, and that many students struggle in history and science classes because they are unable to comprehend their texts effectively. As a report by Carnegie Corporation of New York put it: "Texts read in history class are different from those read in biology, which in turn are substantially different from novels, poems, or essays read in English language arts (ELA). As a result, reading comprehension and writing demands differ across the content areas including ELA."[6]

Taken together, these two additions to standards documents imply that literacy development is no longer the sole province of English language arts teachers. All teachers have the responsibility for developing students' abilities to read, write, speak, and listen. Achieving that goal will require substantial changes in what teachers know and can do, and how schools are structured to develop students' literacy abilities.

Reading

The primary goal of the Common Core State Standards for reading is comprehension, specifically, the ability to comprehend complex texts. The two most critical standards, according to the writers, are Anchor Standard 1 and Anchor Standard 10. Standard 1 states: "Read closely to determine what the text says explicitly and to make logical inferences from it; cite specific textual evidence when writing or speaking to support conclusions drawn from the text." Standard 10 states: "Read and comprehend complex literary and informational texts independently and proficiently." Standards 2 through 9 are intended to be means to those ends (see box 4.1).

The importance of the ability to comprehend complex texts stems from research that shows that this ability is key to college and career readiness. Students who are able to comprehend complex tests are more likely to be successful after high school.[7] However, many students currently lack this ability. The complexity of texts used in colleges has held steady or increased over the past fifty years, while workplace materials and newspapers have also remained at the same level of complexity. The ability to comprehend these texts is critical, though, because, for example, colleges expect students to read independently and to be accountable for their reading.[8]

Yet research also showed that the level of text complexity in high schools has actually declined over time. One study found that the level of difficulty of texts in grade eleven declined substantially between 1963 and 1975, and another study showed that the decline continued through 1991. A more recent study showed that the difference in text complexity between high school and college texts was the equivalent of the difference between grade four and grade eight texts on NAEP.[9]

Moreover, many teachers attempt to make reading and comprehension simpler for students by presenting material via PowerPoint or reading aloud to students. Thus, while texts are not as complex as the texts they will face in college and the workplace, and while texts are even easier than they were in previous years, teachers do not always ask students to read or comprehend their books. Achieving Standard 10 will require major shifts in classroom practice.

In defining text complexity, the Standards suggest that there are three dimensions to the concept. The first is qualitative; this relies on judgments about the levels of meaning or purpose, the structure

BOX 4.1

COMMON CORE ANCHOR STANDARDS FOR READING

Key ideas and details

1. Read closely to determine what the text says explicitly and to make logical inferences from it; cite specific textual evidence when writing or speaking to support conclusions drawn from the text.

2. Determine central ideas or themes of a text and analyze their development; summarize the key supporting details and ideas.

3. Analyze how and why individuals, events, and ideas develop and interact over the course of a text.

Craft and structure

4. Interpret words and phrases as they are used in a text, including determining technical, connotative, and figurative meanings, and analyze how specific word choices shape meaning or tone.

5. Analyze the structure of texts, including how specific sentences, paragraphs, and larger portions of the text (e.g., a section, chapter, scene, or stanza) relate to each other and the whole.

6. Assess how point of view or purpose shapes the content and style of a text.

Integration of knowledge and ideas

7. Integrate and evaluate content presented in diverse formats and media, including visually and quantitatively, as well as in words.

8. Delineate and evaluate the argument and specific claims in a text, including the validity of the reasoning as well as the relevance and sufficiency of the evidence.

9. Analyze how two or more texts address similar themes or topics in order to build knowledge or to compare the approaches the authors take.

Range of reading and level of text complexity

10. Read and comprehend complex literary and informational texts independently and proficiently.

Source: Council of Chief State School Officers and NGA Center for Best Practices, *Common Core State Standards for English Language Arts & Literacy in History/Social Studies, Science, and Technical Subjects* (Washington, DC: Council of Chief State School Officers and NGA Center for Best Practices, 2010).

of the text, the language conventions, and the knowledge demands. The second dimension is quantitative. This refers to the length of words and sentences and is the basis for the familiar "readability formulas." The third dimension relates to the readers themselves and the tasks assigned to them. Teachers must make judgments about a text's appropriateness given students' level of motivation and knowledge, and what students will be expected to demonstrate.

To illustrate the level of text complexity, the quality, and the range of texts the Standards expect, the document includes a list of well-known materials. In grades six through eight, these include literary texts, such as *Little Women, The Adventures of Tom Sawyer*, and Robert Frost's "The Road Not Taken"; as well as nonfiction texts, such as *Narrative of the Life of Frederick Douglass* and John Steinbeck's *Travels with Charlie: In Search of America*. In grades eleven through college and career readiness, the illustrative texts include *Jane Eyre* and *A Raisin in the Sun*, as well as Thomas Paine's *Common Sense*, Richard Wright's *Black Boy*, and George Orwell's "Politics and the English Language."

These suggestions are intended to be illustrative; they do not represent a reading list. The standards writers deliberately avoided creating a reading list at each grade level, recognizing that such a list could become divisive and could detract from the purpose of the Standards, which was to ensure that students are capable of reading increasingly complex texts.

In addition to the emphasis on text complexity, the Common Core State Standards also depart from current practice in the way they define comprehension. As Anchor Standard 1 makes clear, the focus is on close reading to draw evidence from the text. That is, students are expected to demonstrate their comprehension by using what they know from the text to acquire knowledge.

Many state standards and tests took a different approach. Many tests, for example, measured students' abilities to apply the components of comprehension. That is, they asked students to identify the main idea of a passage or to determine the meaning of words in context. Yet these abilities, collectively, did not add up to comprehension; they did not suggest that students are able to "determine what a text says explicitly and make inferences from it," by using evidence from the text. Students who could achieve that standard—those who can comprehend effectively—could perform well on the subskills, like identifying the main idea of a passage. But students who could perform the subskills might not be able to comprehend complex texts.

The Standards also place a greater emphasis than many previous standards and tests on expository texts. Traditionally, literacy instruction has focused primarily on literature and the use of narrative texts. But the standards writers agreed that the demands in college and careers place a greater weight on exposition: Students in most college classes and workers in offices and shops read primarily informational texts, not novels, plays, and poems.

The shift in emphasis toward informational texts corresponds to a shift underway in NAEP. In the 2009 NAEP reading framework, half of the reading passages at grade four are informational, and half are literary; at grade twelve, 70 percent are informational and 30 percent are literary. The Common Core State Standards match these proportions. The Standards document notes that, as a result, much of the reading that students will need to do to meet the Standards will take place in classes other than English language arts; the literacy standards for history/social studies, science, and technical classes also underscore that shift. But, the Standards document also notes, English language arts classes will have to place a greater emphasis than previously on literary nonfiction, as well as on the classic genres of fiction.

To illustrate the kinds of reading students might be expected to do to meet the Standards and the ways they can demonstrate their abilities, the document includes an appendix with excerpts from illustrative texts and sample performance tasks. For example, it suggests that students in grades six through eight could "summarize the development of the morality of Tom Sawyer in Mark Twain's novel of the same name and analyze its connection to themes of accountability and authenticity by noting how it is conveyed through characters, setting, and plot." Students in those grades could also "compare and contrast Laurence Yep's fictional portrayal of Chinese immigrants in turn-of-the-twentieth-century San Francisco in *Dragonwings* to historical accounts of the same period (using materials detailing the 1906 San Francisco earthquake) in order to glean a deeper understanding of how authors use or alter historical sources to create a sense of time and place as well as make fictional characters lifelike and real."[10]

Writing

Like the reading standards, the writing standards also imply some significant shifts from current practice. One of the most important is a reduced emphasis on narrative writing and a greater emphasis on informational and explanatory writing. Personal narratives are a staple of schooling ("How I Spent My Summer Vacation"), but except for the essays students write to apply to college, students seldom write personal narratives in college or the workplace. Informational writing, in which authors attempt to explain something or inform others about a topic, is much more prevalent. The Standards' expectations match those of the 2009 NAEP framework, in which about a third of the items at grades four and eight involve writing to persuade, a third involve writing to explain, and a third involve writing to convey experience. In twelfth grade, however, 40 percent of the writing tasks involve writing to persuade, 40 percent involve writing to explain, and only 20 percent involve writing to convey experience (see box 4.2).

The Standards also differ from conventional practice in the area of persuasive writing. Typically, such writing involves the expression of an opinion—consider the common task of writing to the principal to suggest changing a school rule. The Standards, on the other hand, require students to develop the ability to make logical arguments. They are expected to appeal to reason, rather than to emotion, and to take into account the positions of potential opponents. Most importantly, they are expected to draw on evidence, just as students are expected to do to meet the reading standards.

To illustrate the kinds of writing that meet the standards, the document includes an appendix with samples of student work,

BOX 4.2

COMMON CORE ANCHOR STANDARDS FOR WRITING

Text types and purposes

1. Write arguments to support claims in an analysis of substantive topics or texts, using valid reasoning and relevant and sufficient evidence.

2. Write informative/explanatory texts to examine and convey complex ideas and information clearly and accurately through the effective selection, organization, and analysis of content.

3. Write narratives to develop real or imagined experiences or events using effective technique, well-chosen details, and well-structured event sequences.

Production and distribution of writing

4. Produce clear and coherent writing in which the development, organization, and style are appropriate to task, purpose, and audience.

5. Develop and strengthen writing as needed by planning, revising, editing, rewriting, or trying a new approach.

6. Use technology, including the Internet, to produce and publish writing and to interact and collaborate with others.

Research to build and present knowledge

7. Conduct short as well as more sustained research projects based on focused questions, demonstrating understanding of the subject under investigation.

8. Gather relevant information from multiple print and digital sources, assess the credibility and accuracy of each source, and integrate the information while avoiding plagiarism.

9. Draw evidence from literary or informational texts to support analysis, reflection, and research.

Range of writing

10. Write routinely over extended time frames (time for research, reflection, and revision) and shorter time frames (a single sitting or a day or two) for a range of tasks, purposes, and audiences.

Source: Council of Chief State School Officers and NGA Center for Best Practices, *Common Core State Standards for English Language Arts & Literacy in History/Social Studies, Science, and Technical Subjects* (Washington, DC: Council of Chief State School Officers and NGA Center for Best Practices, 2010).

along with annotations that show why the work is exemplary. For example, the appendix includes a first grader's informational report about Spain, entitled "My Big Book about Spain." In this report, the appendix states, the writer names the topic, supplies some facts about the topic, provides some sense of closure ("One day when I am a researcher I am going to go to Spain and write about it!"), and demonstrates command of some of the conventions of standard English.

An informative/expository essay by a ninth grader, meanwhile, compares and contrasts Sandra Cisneros's novel *The House on Mango Street* and the film *Whale Rider*, directed by Niki Caro. The writer, the document explains, introduces the topic; organizes complex ideas, concepts, and information to make important connections and distinctions; develops the topic with well-chosen, relevant, and sufficient facts; uses appropriate and varied transitions; uses precise language and domain-specific vocabulary; establishes and maintains a formal style and objective tone; provides a concluding section that follows from and supports the information presented; and demonstrates exemplary command of the conventions of standard written English.

Speaking and Listening

The standards for speaking and listening are in two broad categories: comprehension and collaboration, and presentation of knowledge and ideas (see box 4.3). While the former appears to address listening and the latter addresses speaking, each category addresses both speaking and listening. For example, an anchor standard for comprehension and collaboration states: "Prepare for and participate effectively in a range of conversations and collaborations with diverse partners, building on others' ideas and expressing their own clearly and persuasively." Likewise, an anchor standard for presentation of knowledge and ideas states: "Make strategic use of digital media and visual displays of data to express information and enhance *understanding* of presentations" (emphasis added).

BOX 4.3

COMMON CORE ANCHOR STANDARDS FOR SPEAKING AND LISTENING

Comprehension and collaboration

1. Prepare for and participate effectively in a range of conversations and collaborations with diverse partners, building on others' ideas and expressing their own clearly and persuasively.

2. Integrate and evaluate information presented in diverse media and formats, including visually, quantitatively, and orally.

3. Evaluate a speaker's point of view, reasoning, and use of evidence and rhetoric.

Presentation of knowledge and ideas

4. Present information, findings, and supporting evidence such that listeners can follow the line of reasoning and the organization, development, and style are appropriate to task, purpose, and audience.

5. Make strategic use of digital media and visual displays of data to express information and enhance understanding of presentations.

6. Adapt speech to a variety of contexts and communicative tasks, demonstrating command of formal English when indicated or appropriate.

Source: Council of Chief State School Officers and NGA Center for Best Practices, *Common Core State Standards for English Language Arts & Literacy in History/Social Studies, Science, and Technical Subjects* (Washington, DC: Council of Chief State School Officers and NGA Center for Best Practices, 2010).

The document notes that students should have opportunities to participate in a range of speaking and listening experiences, including one-on-one with a partner, in small groups, and in whole-class discussions. And it notes that digital media have broadened and expanded the role of speaking and listening in acquiring and sharing knowledge, and suggests that these media enable students to speak and listen in a variety of new ways, such as through embedded video and audio.

Language

While the Standards place a strong emphasis on the comprehension of increasingly complex texts and the ability to write using evidence, the Standards do not neglect language use. Indeed, the document notes, college and career readiness demands that students have control over grammar and usage, and that they must be able to determine or clarify the meaning of grade-appropriate words. The standards for language therefore address the conventions of standard English, knowledge of language, and vocabulary acquisition and use. (Standards for knowledge of language begin in grade two; see box 4.4.)

The document notes, however, that the inclusion of a separate strand of language standards does not suggest that conventions and vocabulary are unrelated to reading, writing, speaking, and listening. On the contrary, it states; they are "inseparable."

MATHEMATICS STANDARDS

The goal of the mathematics standards is spelled out on the first page of the document: focus and coherence. The evidence from international studies suggested that, compared to standards from high-performing countries, U.S. standards were "a mile wide and an inch deep": they included a large number of topics without getting into any in depth. As a result, students did not learn to understand mathematics concepts and performed far less well than students in other countries that focused their instruction in coherent way.[11]

To provide focus and coherence, the standards writers concentrated on the topics that were most important for students to learn and left out peripheral topics. To achieve coherence, the standards laid out a logical sequence of student learning from grade to grade that was intended to lead to college and career readiness by the end of high school.

The mathematics standards are in two parts. The first are standards for mathematical content, which are the traditional topical

---

BOX 4.4

COMMON CORE ANCHOR STANDARDS FOR LANGUAGE

Conventions of standard English

1. Demonstrate command of the conventions of standard English grammar and usage when writing or speaking.

2. Demonstrate command of the conventions of standard English capitalization, punctuation, and spelling when writing.

Knowledge of language

3. Apply knowledge of language to understand how language functions in different contexts, to make effective choices for meaning or style, and to comprehend more fully when reading or listening.

Vocabulary acquisition and use

4. Determine or clarify the meaning of unknown and multiple-meaning words and phrases by using context clues, analyzing meaningful word parts, and consulting general and specialized reference materials, as appropriate.

5. Demonstrate understanding of word relationships and nuances in word meanings.

6. Acquire and use accurately a range of general academic and domain-specific words and phrases sufficient for reading, writing, speaking, and listening at the college and career readiness level; demonstrate independence in gathering vocabulary knowledge when considering a word or phrase important to comprehension or expression.

Source: Council of Chief State School Officers and NGA Center for Best Practices, *Common Core State Standards for English Language Arts & Literacy in History/Social Studies, Science, and Technical Subjects* (Washington, DC: Council of Chief State School Officers and NGA Center for Best Practices, 2010).

---

areas: numbers and operations, algebra, functions, statistics and probability, and geometry. The second are standards for mathematical practices. These "describe varieties of expertise that mathematics educators at all levels should seek to develop in their students. These practices rest on important 'processes and proficiencies' with longstanding importance in mathematics education."[12]

The standards for mathematical practice are:

1. "Make sense of problems and persevere in solving them."
2. "Reason abstractly and quantitatively."
3. "Construct viable arguments and critique the reasoning of others."
4. "Model with mathematics."
5. "Use appropriate tools strategically."
6. "Attend to precision."
7. "Look for and make use of structure."
8. "Look for and express regularity in repeated reasoning."

The Standards do not state how to connect the standards for practice to the standards for content, although the document states that designers of curriculum, assessments, and professional development should attend to the connections. For example, it suggests, assessments might ask students to understand particular concepts by asking them to represent problems coherently, use tools strategically, and explain mathematics accurately to other students in order to demonstrate their understanding.

Standards in K–5

Like the English language arts standards, the mathematics standards in many ways represent a departure from typical practice. These variations are evident in the standards for the early grades. There, the emphasis is clear: the focus is squarely on arithmetic.

Of course, arithmetic has always been a pillar of elementary mathematics instruction. But elementary classrooms have also devoted class time to many other topics as well, such as time (clocks and calendars), money, and data. While these topics might be useful, they are not fundamental to the mathematics students need in order to graduate from high school ready for college and careers. Moreover, the inclusion of multiple topics has meant that students have had too little time to learn the concepts that are truly fundamental. In order to provide the focus and coherence that high-performing countries offer in their standards, the standards writers pared down elementary mathematics to concentrate on arithmetic.

In doing so, however, the Standards make clear that arithmetic is a lot more than a matter of adding and subtracting columns of numbers. As the document notes, arithmetic is the foundation for algebraic thinking. Thus, the emphasis is on a few key topics that provide fundamental underpinnings to more advanced mathematics, such as place value and fractions. In addition, the Standards expect students to demonstrate that they understand key concepts, not just that they can perform operations. For example, second graders are expected to "explain why addition and subtraction strategies work, using place value and the properties of operations."[13]

At the same time, the Standards expect students to develop fluency in basic operations. By the end of third grade, students should know the multiplication tables. And while the Standards do not explicitly call for or prohibit the use of calculators, the practice standard that states that students should use appropriate tools strategically notes that "appropriate tools" include pencil and paper.

While the focus in the elementary grades is on arithmetic, the Standards in kindergarten through grade five also include expectations for geometry and, to a lesser extent, data, but these receive less emphasis than arithmetic. The Standards at those grade levels do not include statistics and probability, however, a controversial topic within the mathematics education community at those grade levels. But the Standards do include material that is fundamental to an early understanding of statistics and probability, such as ratio and proportion.

Grades Six through Eight

In the middle grades, the Standards call for the introduction of additional topics. But, unlike many previous standards, these new topics build on those in previous grades; they do not simply repeat topics introduced earlier. The Standards assume that students have learned what was expected in prior grades.

One new topic is statistics. Statistics is important because data are a ubiquitous feature of life in the twenty-first century. But, as the Standards show, statistics is intended to build on students' prior understanding of number. Students are expected to understand the distribution of data and know that the way the distribution is represented (mean, median, mode) depends on how it is measured. This expectation—that students understand distribution—varies considerably from traditional practice, where students typically calculate means, medians, and modes without necessarily understanding how they represent the distribution of data.

Middle school mathematics also introduces algebra topics. In sixth grade, students are expected to understand the use of variables in mathematical expressions. Specifically, they are expected to "write, read, and evaluate expressions in which letters stand for numbers." In addition, students are expected to "use variables to represent numbers and write expressions when solving a real world or mathematical problem; understand that a variable can represent an unknown number, or, depending on the purpose at hand, any number in a specified set."[14]

In seventh grade, students are expected to "use variables to represent quantities in a real-world or mathematical problem, and construct simple equations and inequalities to solve problems by reasoning about the quantities."[15] That is, students should know how to form equations and inequalities based on real-world situations, such as determining the width of a rectangle when the perimeter and length are known.

Introducing algebraic concepts in sixth and seventh grade makes it possible for students to take algebra 1 in eighth grade. In recent years, many districts have tried to increase the number of students who take algebra in eighth grade, so that they could take more advanced mathematics in high school. The Common Core State Standards do not mandate algebra in eighth grade. In fact, the Standards for eighth grade include geometry concepts, specifically, an understanding of the Pythagorean Theorem. However, they include enough of the prerequisites for algebra so that students would be prepared to take algebra 1 in eighth grade.

As we will see in chapter 5, California educators did not feel the Standards went far enough and they added content to earlier grades so that in their view, all students would be able to take algebra in eighth grade. But other states felt the preparation was sufficient.

High School Standards

The high school mathematics standards represent a significant shift from those in early grades. In contrast to the grade-by-grade standards for kindergarten through eighth grade, the high school mathematics standards are organized by six conceptual categories, specifically: number and quantity; algebra; functions; modeling; geometry; and statistics and probability.

This organization reflects the fact that states vary widely in how they organize mathematics instruction in high schools. Some states use a traditional approach, with separate courses for algebra 1, geometry, algebra 2, trigonometry, and so forth. Other states, however, use integrated mathematics courses that include content from various mathematics subdisciplines. The organization of the Standards can accommodate both approaches.

Modeling is a special case. Modeling is a standard of mathematical practice, rather than content, but the inclusion of modeling in the high school standards shows that the standards writers consider it a central feature of mathematics at the high school level. Modeling is, essentially, using mathematical thinking to analyze real-world situations and make appropriate decisions. In business, for example, few people are asked to solve an equation that is already written. But workers frequently have to examine data and come up with ways to make sense of them and produce solutions, such as determining the cost of an item by relating unit price and quantity. As the Standards state, modeling is "the process of choosing and using appropriate mathematics and statistics to analyze empirical situations, to understand them better, and to improve decisions."[16]

The high school mathematics standards are intended for all students and represent the threshold level necessary for college and career readiness. In fact, as the document notes, most research on college and career readiness suggests that much of the mathematics necessary for postsecondary success is taught in grades six through eight. This includes applying ratio reasoning in solving problems, computing fluently with fractions and decimals, and solving problems involving angle measure, surface area, and volume. Assessments to measure students' readiness for college and careers should include these concepts, the Standards note.

However, the Standards also include content that students would need to know if they intend to pursue higher-level mathematics, such as calculus, discrete mathematics, or advanced statistics. This content is designated with a special symbol (+).

While the standards document itself is agnostic about the type of course sequence states and districts should use in high school, the document also includes an appendix that outlines four pathways for organizing the Standards into course sequences. The pathways are:

- A traditional sequence that includes two algebra courses and a geometry course, with data, statistics, and probability included in each
- An integrated sequence that consists of three courses, each of which includes number, algebra, geometry, data, statistics, and probability
- A "compacted" version of the traditional sequence in which students complete the content in seventh grade, eighth grade, and high school algebra 1 in seventh and eighth grade, in order to be on track to take calculus or other college-level courses in twelfth grade
- A "compacted" version of the integrated sequence in which students complete the content of seventh grade, eighth grade, and high school mathematics 1 in seventh and eighth grade, in order to be on track to take calculus or other college-level courses in twelfth grade

The document notes that, traditionally, districts have devoted more resources—such as experienced teachers and higher-quality materials—to the accelerated pathways. But, it argues, all pathways should get the same attention to resources and materials that the accelerated pathways currently receive. All students should be able to choose whatever pathway they want, according to their interests, and all should put students on track toward college and career readiness.

In addition, the document notes that not all students progress at the same pace and that some students might need additional support in order to be ready for college and careers at the end of high school. Such students should have access to tutoring, extended class time, or additional instruction during the summer. Placing such students in lower-level mathematics classes should not be an option, the document states. Such classes make it impossible for students to be ready for colleges and careers by the time they graduate from high school, it notes. "Watered-down courses which leave students uninspired to learn, unable to catch up to their peers and unready for success in postsecondary courses or for entry into many skilled professions upon graduation from high school are neither necessary nor desirable," the document states.[17]

THE FUTURE OF THE STANDARDS

While the standards writers based their decisions about which topics to include and when on evidence about college and career readiness, the research base is not rock solid in every case. In the cases where the research was slight or ambiguous, the writers used the best available evidence. As noted in chapter 3, the validation committee, a panel of experts and practitioners appointed by the Council of Chief State School Officers and the National Governors Association, concluded that the document did in fact reflect available research on college and career readiness, as well as international benchmarks.

Once the Standards are implemented, researchers must examine them to determine if they are indeed valid: if a student who meets the Standards is in fact prepared for postsecondary success. Once this research is available, it is likely the Standards will be revised, with some standards considered less important and additional standards perhaps added. For this to happen, though, the Standards have to first be adopted.

5

FORTY-THREE AND COUNTING

The Road to Adoption

OFFICIALS IN KENTUCKY DID NOT WAIT for the writers of the Common Core State Standards to finish their deliberations before deciding to adopt them as their own. In February 2010, a month before draft standards were released for comment and four months before the final version would be unveiled, the Kentucky State Board of Education voted unanimously to adopt the standards in English language arts and mathematics, the first state to do so.

The board then went a step further. It met with the boards that oversee teacher licensure and public higher education and adopted a resolution to incorporate the Common Core State Standards in their own standards. The goal was to create alignment among teacher education, K–12 instruction, and postsecondary education—exactly what proponents of standards-based reform have been advocating for decades.

Technically, the board's vote on the Standards was conditional; they put off regulatory review of the decision until after the final version was published. But the enthusiasm with which state officials greeted the Standards left little doubt that they would hold onto their position as first out of the box in adoption. Governor Stephen L. Beshear and the chairs of the legislature's education committees attended the board meeting to express their support, and the president of the state teachers' association also backed the move.

In fact, the officials had prepared for this action for months. In 2009, the legislature passed a bill requiring the state to revise its K–12 academic standards in 2010 and to begin the process of revising its state tests. The law also required the board that oversees public higher education, the Council on Postsecondary Education, to sign an agreement stating the content standards in reading and mathematics would be aligned with postsecondary course standards in those subjects, and required the Education Professional Standards Board to train teacher education faculty on the Standards. To fulfill the requirement, the board studied draft Common Core State Standards that were circulated among states for review.

Perhaps it was not a coincidence that Kentucky would be poised to become the first state to adopt the Common Core State Standards. Gene Wilhoit, the executive director of the Council of Chief State School Officers, one of the two organizations that led the Common Core State Standards effort, had served as state commissioner of education in the Bluegrass State from 2000 to 2006.

Dozens of other states would soon follow Kentucky's lead. The speed with which states adopted the Common Core State Standards suggests that they were widely accepted. But the process was not seamless, and it came about with the behind-the-scenes help of a number of national organizations.

STANDARDS ADOPTION

The adoption process was different from any that had taken place in the past twenty years. Previously, states adopted their own standards. Typically, state agencies created committees of educators and public officials, who came up with their own definitions of what students should know and be able to do. These efforts were designed to get buy-in for the standards; if many people were involved in developing the standards, more people would accept them.

In many cases, states set up standards commissions, which would weigh public input and study materials about the subject areas and come up with recommendations for standards. The state board of education, in most cases, would have the final say. (Minnesota and Wisconsin have no state boards of education.) In some states, such as Maine, the legislature also has to approve the standards. The board's vote is not a rubber stamp; in Kansas, for example, the board's action to remove the word *evolution* from state standards, as recounted in chapter 2, overturned a decision by the state's standards commission.

The state-led process might have achieved its goal of building support and ownership of the standards, but it also attracted criticism. Commentators noted that the process of building consensus led to compromise and logrolling, and the result was often a vague set of standards intended not to offend anyone or a voluminous list of topics that included everything in order to make everyone happy. Such standards often lacked coherence and were not tied to any research-based theories about how students learn a subject area.

In the early days of the standards movement, Governor Roy Romer of Colorado, a champion of the effort, repeatedly urged states simply to adopt national standards, such as the mathematics standards developed by the National Council of Teachers of Mathematics. But states did not take him up on the suggestion, instead preferring to build their own standards. One exception was the District of Columbia, where in 2005, Clifford Janey, the superintendent, persuaded the board to adopt the Massachusetts standards in English language arts and mathematics. Janey had been chief academic officer of the Boston Public Schools, and the Massachusetts standards were highly regarded as among the best in the country.

To get states to adopt the Common Core State Standards, then, advocates would have to convince boards and other policy makers to operate differently. And they laid down clear parameters for their decisions: the National Governors Association (NGA) and the Council of Chief State School Officers (CCSSO) insisted that states had to adopt the standards whole; they could not pick and choose among them. Otherwise the Standards would lose their coherence, and they would not be comparable from state to state. However, the groups said that states could add 15 percent above the common core. The CCSSO and NGA did not define this guideline—or who would measure whether in fact states added no more than 15 per-cent—but states interpreted the language to mean that they could include content important to them that was not included in the Common Core State Standards. In the end, only three states made significant additions.

In seeking adoption from the state boards, leaders of the standards effort also had to persuade the boards to change their calendars in some cases. Many states had schedules for revising their standards, some spelled out in state law, and some states had adopted revised standards only recently. Kentucky's 2009 law was aimed at enabling that state to adopt the Common Core State Standards in 2010, but other states had to change their schedules.

States had a powerful incentive to do so, however. As noted in chapter 1, the U.S. Department of Education's Race to the Top program, which provided $4.3 billion in grants to states to pursue reforms, awarded states forty points out of a possible five hundred if they agreed to adopt, by August 2, 2010, common standards that were internationally benchmarked and that prepared students for college and careers. The deadline for applications for phase one of the competition was January 19, 2010, and forty states and the District of Columbia applied. All but one state said they would commit to adopting the Common Core State Standards, and all but six states provided a specific timetable for adoption.[1]

Whether Race to the Top caused states to agree to adopt the Common Core State Standards or whether the program provided an additional incentive and affected the timing of adoption remains a subject of debate. A survey of state officials by the Center on Education Policy found that twenty-seven states said federal encouragement, such as Race to the Top, helped their decision to adopt the Common Core State Standards. But respondents in two states said the federal actions hurt their decision, and eight states said it made no difference. But more state officials said the rigor of the Common Core State Standards was a bigger factor in their decision to adopt them.[2]

For his part, President Obama has said he thinks Race to the Top made a difference. In his 2011 State of the Union Address, he remarked: "Race to the Top is the most meaningful reform of our public schools in a generation. For less than 1 percent of what we spend on education each year, it has led over 40 states to raise their standards for teaching and learning."[3]

The Obama administration also floated the idea of exerting more federal control over the adoption of standards. In February 2010, at a meeting of the NGA, Obama suggested that he would propose requiring states to adopt the Common Core State Standards as a condition of receiving federal Title I dollars. That idea sent shivers down the spines of critics who opposed too much federal involvement in education. Neal McCluskey, associate director of the Cato Institute's Center for Educational Freedom, called the idea "federally extorted standardization,"[4] and Anne L. Bryant, the executive director of the National School Boards Association, said it amounted to "an unnecessary over-reach by the federal government to coerce states to adopt a particular approach or be shut out of future funding for key programs." Bryant went on to point out that "[t]his level of coercion is unnecessary, because forty-eight states are already voluntarily working to develop common core standards."[5]

The administration backed off from its proposal somewhat. In its blueprint for a reauthorization of the Elementary and Secondary Education Act, the administration proposed requiring states to set standards for college and career readiness; adopting the Common Core State Standards would be one way states could show they had done so. Otherwise, a state's four-year university system could certify that a state's standards prepare students for postsecondary education.

The issue did not entirely go away, however. Members of the emerging Tea Party movement, who supported a more limited role for the federal government, charged that the Common Core State Standards represented an Obama-led "federal takeover" of local schools, much as they claimed that the health-care reform law was a federal takeover of health insurance. Their claims about the standards, at least, were unfounded, however. The standards effort had begun before President Obama was elected, and each state had made a decision on whether to adopt the standards on its own. The effort was and continues to be (as of this writing) state-run and state-directed.

STATE DECISIONS, NATIONAL ADVOCACY

While state boards of education weighed their decisions, national organizations, many of which were funded by the Bill & Melinda Gates Foundation, met regularly to strategize about ways to support state adoption of the Standards and develop materials to advocate on their behalf. The organizations included Achieve, the Alliance for Excellent Education, the Campaign for High School Equity (a coalition of civil-rights organizations), the Council of State Governments, the James B. Hunt, Jr. Institute for Educational Leadership and Policy, and the National Association of State Boards of Education (NASBE).[6] The groups held regular conference calls to consider the status of adoption and highlight states where assistance might be needed. They commissioned a poll to gauge public reaction to the proposed Standards and identify language that might be effective in soliciting support.

The groups also produced materials to help support adoption. For example, the Alliance for Excellent Education produced a policy brief entitled "Common Standards: The Time Is Now" to make the case for the Standards, and developed and distributed "state cards" that indicated the current status of the Standards in each state.[7] It distributed these materials widely and made them available to the other organizations in their advocacy efforts.

Likewise, the Campaign for High School Equity (CHSE) produced a brief that highlighted the importance of common standards for students of color.[8] The Alliance and CHSE later held a meeting with about a hundred representatives of CHSE-affiliated organizations to consider issues in standards implementation that might affect communities of color.

The Hunt Institute worked with the National Research Council to conduct workshops to examine research on standards and assessments. The first workshop provided evidence of the wide variations in standards among states and helped bolster the case for common standards. The second workshop explored new directions in assessment and suggested ways that common assessments could measure a broader set of knowledge and skills than conventional tests tended to do.

The Council of State Governments (CSG) and NASBE, meanwhile, held regional forums to inform their members about the Standards and enable them to ask questions of leaders involved in the effort. While the CSG meetings provided basic information to state legislators, the NASBE meetings were critical to help inform the policy makers who would be voting whether or not to adopt the Standards.

The organizations also pulled in some high-profile individuals to help in the advocacy efforts. For example, after Governor Tim Pawlenty of Minnesota expressed concerns about the Common Core mathematics standards, Governor James Hunt, Jr., president of the Hunt Institute, met with standards writers to get a better understanding of what the Standards called for and called Pawlenty, a member of the institute's board, to discuss the issue.[9] Although Minnesota did not adopt the mathematics standards, arguing that its own standards were superior to the Common Core, it did adopt the standards for English language arts.

STATE ADOPTIONS PILE UP

Meanwhile, state boards continued to adopt the standards. In May, a month before the final version of the Standards was released, three states gave them tentative approval: Hawaii, Maryland, and West Virginia. In each case, approval was technically conditional, so that the board could review the final version of the document. All of the states applied for the Race to the Top program.

In June, once the Standards were released, adoptions came fast and furious, especially since the August 2 deadline for adoption set by the Race to the Top program loomed. Thirteen states adopted the Standards in June, and another fourteen and the District of Columbia followed suit in July.

A few state boards took the unusual step of changing their meeting schedules in order to vote to adopt the Standards before August 2. In Florida, for example, the board discussed the Standards at a June 15 meeting but did not have another meeting scheduled until September, so members held a conference call on July 27 to vote to adopt the Standards. In Georgia, Missouri, and Nevada, board members moved their meetings up from August.

Several states also changed their schedules for adopting standards in order to consider the Common Core State Standards. In Ohio, for example, the state legislature in 2009 passed a measure requiring that the state board of education revise academic standards to incorporate twenty-first century skills and to do so by June 2010. Working groups appointed by the state department of education began drafting new standards in English language arts, mathematics, science, and social studies. They submitted the drafts of the science and social studies standards for review in November 2009, but held back the English language arts and mathematics standards in order to wait for the Common Core. The state board adopted the Common Core State Standards on June 7.

Similarly, Florida also had a legislative mandate to revise its standards and began the process of developing the Next Generation Sunshine State Standards in 2008. But the work was put on hold when the Common Core State Standards development got under way. The department then conducted an analysis comparing the draft Next Generation Sunshine State Standards with the Common Core State Standards and, after finding the two documents comparable, the state board adopted the Standards on July 27, 2010. The department then proposed several additions to the Standards, and the board adopted the complete set in December.

State leaders expressed their strong beliefs that adopting the Common Core State Standards was an essential step in educational improvement. In Tennessee, for example, former U.S. Senator Bill Frist, who headed an education reform support organization known as the State Collaborative on Reforming Education (SCORE), said the state had been publicly embarrassed by national reports published in 2007 that showed that its standards were too low. In response, he said, Governor Phil Bredesen built a bipartisan coalition in the legislature in favor of higher standards, and SCORE held more than eighty town hall meetings across the state over a two-year period to discuss the need for reform. "So when the time came in July 2010 to decide whether or not to adopt the Common Core standards, the State Board of Education's decision was easy," Frist wrote on a Web site created by Carnegie Corporation of New York to support improvement in science and mathematics. "Tennessee already had come a long way since its failing grade in 2007. With both political and business leadership aligned, it approached educational reform in a nonpartisan way."[10]

Likewise, Florida had also received low marks from national reports on the quality of its standards. In 2007, the state went through the process of revising them and then became an enthusiastic partner in the Common Core effort, according to Commissioner of Education Eric Smith:

> As the standards emerged, we came to understand the benefits of signing on and the value of having our students compete with others around the nation and around the world. And, because of bipartisan state support, an understanding of the connection between education and our economic future, and the rigor of the Common Core standards, there was not much state opposition to adoption. We fully expect that the Common Core standards will enable us to compare our students with those in other states, and that we will be better able to benchmark our achievement with international standards. We feel these comparisons will help us to better serve our students in a competitive, global economy.[11]

State officials also said that they adopted the Standards because they were impressed with their quality and recognized that they were stronger than their own state standards. The standards writers made repeated efforts to meet with state leaders and go over the Standards in order to show the similarities and differences between state standards and the Common Core; these efforts paid off.

At the same time, the fact that the Standards were intended to be *common* also made it easier for states to adopt them. For some states with relatively low standards, higher standards—that might put them in a bad light if fewer students were able to meet them at first—would be a hard sell. But when most of the states jumped into the pool at the same time, states were more likely to join. They had political cover. And the common standards offered the prospect of cost savings: if states could pool their money to build assessments and develop curricula, they could reduce some expenditures at a time when budgets were tight. The experience of the New England Common Assessment Program (NECAP), which enabled three small states to develop a high-quality assessment collectively that none could develop on their own proved enticing.

DEBATES ERUPT

Because of this strong support, the board debates on the Standards in many states elicited little vocal opposition, and for the most part, the board votes were unanimous. In many cases, the boards took action with very little publicity.

Not so in Massachusetts. That state had a richly deserved reputation for the quality and effectiveness of its standards. The English language arts standards earned a grade of A– from the Thomas B. Fordham Institute, one of the highest grades of any state, and the mathematics standards had earned a B+.[12] As noted earlier, the Massachusetts standards were the only ones to be adopted by another state, when the District of Columbia chose them as its own.

Moreover, the standards appeared to get results. Massachusetts has consistently been the highest-performing state on NAEP. In 2009, nearly half—47 percent—of Massachusetts fourth graders performed at the proficient level or above in reading, more than any other state and far more than the 31 percent who performed at that level nationally. Forty-two percent of eighth graders performed at the proficient level or above in reading; only Connecticut matched that level.[13]

In mathematics, 57 percent of Massachusetts fourth graders performed at the proficient level or above, compared with 39 percent nationally, and 51 percent of eighth graders reached that level, compared with 32 percent nationally.[14]

The Bay State's standards, therefore, had a lot of support, and a number of people within the state were reluctant to change them, especially if it appeared that the replacement would be less rigorous than the current standards. Two key architects of the state's education reforms, former Governor William Weld and former state senate president Thomas Birmingham, had taken that view. But two former state commissioners of education, David Driscoll and Robert Antonucci, backed the Common Core State Standards.

The debate turned political. Republicans, including Senate Minority Leader Richard Tisei, accused Governor Deval Patrick, a Democrat who said he would adopt Common Core if it did not lower standards, of attempting to eliminate the state's own test, the Massachusetts Comprehensive Assessment System (MCAS), to curry favor with teacher unions, which opposed the test. The debate became an issue in Patrick's reelection campaign as well. But Patrick maintained that the state would keep the test and would only have to make minor modifications to it to conform to the Common Core State Standards.

Patrick and his aides also cited studies from outside organizations, including the Fordham Institute, that showed that the Common Core State Standards were stronger than the Massachusetts standards. The state's Business Alliance for Education, a supporter of the Common Core State Standards, commissioned a study by WestEd, a federally funded research laboratory based in San Francisco, to compare the state's standards to the Common Core; the review found considerable overlap in content coverage and that the two sets of standards were comparable in clarity and measurability. But advocates of the Massachusetts standards conducted a study of their own (along with a study comparing California's standards to the Common Core) that came to the opposite conclusion. The study, by the Pioneer Institute, a conservative Boston-based policy organization, contended that the Common Core English language arts standards were less specific about the literary content students are expected to learn than Massachusetts' standards, and that the mathematics standards omitted significant topics like the geometry of circles and chords, complex numbers, and logarithms, that were included in Massachusetts' standards.[15]

In the end, though, the state board voted to adopt the Common Core State Standards, with all members present voting in favor.

Two members who had been critical of the Common Core, Thomas Fortmann and Sandra Stotsky, who had coauthored the Pioneer Institute report, did not attend the meeting. Shortly after the vote, Governor Patrick declined to reappoint Fortmann and Stotsky to the board, a move the *Boston Globe* called a "purge."[16]

A similar battle was heating up in California. That state's standards were even more highly regarded than those in Massachusetts—both its English language arts and mathematics standards earned an A from the Fordham Institute—but its performance on NAEP was among the lowest in the country.[17]

Nevertheless, many educators in California did not want to adopt weaker standards, and a contentious debate broke out among members of the state's twenty-one-member academic standards commission, a panel appointed by Governor Arnold Schwarzenegger and legislative leaders to analyze the Common Core State Standards and decide whether to recommend adoption by the state board of education. In a meeting that lasted until midnight, the commission pored over the Common Core State Standards and made a number of modifications to the English language arts standards. However, in keeping with the ground rules established by the NGA and the CCSSO, the commission added components of its state standards to the Standards; the panel did not delete any standards.

The real battle erupted in mathematics. There, Schwarzenegger, who had appointed a majority of the commission, had insisted that the standards include algebra 1 in eighth grade. (As noted in chapter 4, the Common Core State Standards include algebra concepts in eighth and ninth grades.) To accommodate that demand, the commission shifted some of the Common Core standards to earlier grades to prepare students for algebra in eighth grade.

However, two members of the commission, Bill Evers and Ze'ev Wurman (a coauthor of the Pioneer Institute report that criticized the Common Core State Standards), repeatedly sought to replace the Common Core mathematics standards with those of California, which they had helped write. They offered numerous amendments, extending the meeting well past its scheduled 3 P.M. adjournment time, and were defeated every time. The commission finally voted fourteen to two (Evers and Wurman were the dissenters) to adopt the amended Common Core State Standards, and the state board adopted them unanimously on August 2.

The adoption vote also proved controversial in Colorado. There, the issue was over local control. Like many western states, Colorado is leery of national and especially federal involvement in its affairs, and many of the speakers who showed up during the state board's consideration of the Common Core State Standards expressed the view that Colorado's standards should be set by Coloradans. In the end, the board voted four to three to adopt the Standards.

SOME OPPOSITION EMERGES

By August 2, the deadline set by Race to the Top, thirty-four states had adopted the Common Core State Standards, and Indiana joined the pack the following day. Vermont and Delaware added their votes later that month. Two-thirds of the country, including almost all of the largest states, had adopted the standards, meaning that the vast majority of students would be held to the same expectations in English language arts and mathematics.

An influential report that came out in July 2010 suggested that most students were better off with these state decisions. The Fordham Institute, which had been rating state standards since 1997, published a report that rated state standards and compared them with the Common Core State Standards. The report gave the Common Core State Standards an A– in mathematics and a B+ in English language arts. It concluded that the Standards were superior in clarity and rigor to the mathematics standards in thirty-nine states, and superior in clarity and rigor to the English language arts standards in thirty-seven states. The Common Core outranked standards in both subjects in thirty-three states. In only three states were state English language arts standards superior to the Common Core: California, the District of Columbia, and Indiana, and all of those had adopted the Standards. In eleven states, the comparison was "too close to call," the report concluded.[18]

113

Despite that vote of confidence, it was unlikely that standards would be adopted in every state. Two states, Alaska and Texas, opted out of the process altogether and did not even participate in the development of the document. The Texas State Board of Education underscored the opposition to the effort in a statement issued January 15, 2010, in which the board stated: "Any attempt to impose a national curriculum and testing system is a likely precursor to a federal takeover of public schools."

Virginia, originally a party to the agreement, dropped out in May 2010. The original memorandum of agreement to take part in the Common Core State Standards effort was signed by a Democrat, Governor Tim Kaine, but in 2009, Virginians elected a Republican, Robert McDonnell, and although the state applied for the first round of the Race to the Top competition, McDonnell announced that Virginia would not apply for the second round of the program because of the preference for common standards. As McDonnell explained, "We can't go back. We've been working on this for 15 years. Our standards are much superior. They're well accepted. They're validated. All the education leaders have a comfort level with those. So once again, a federal mandate to adopt a federal common core standard is just not something I can accept, nor can most of the education leaders in Virginia, nor can most of the legislators."[19]

Nevertheless, Virginia state officials say they are adjusting their standards to align with the Common Core. The state is adding content to its mathematics standards to match the Common Core State Standards expectations and is revising its state mathematics test to reflect those changes. The new test is expected to be introduced in 2011–2012.

Minnesota also declined to adopt the Common Core mathematics standards. In a letter to the leaders of the Smarter Balanced Assessment Consortium, one of the two state groups that are developing assessments to measure the Standards, Pawlenty stated that the mathematics standards "did not meet our expectations." He said the state would not join the consortium, because consortium members would have to adopt the standards to do so. The governor added, though, that Minnesota would conduct an analysis comparing the state mathematics standards and the Common Core State Standards in 2011, and that the legislature would consider revising its standards. Minnesota did, however, adopt the Common Core English language arts standards in September 2010. The state was the only one to adopt the Common Core State Standards for only one subject.

Some backlash to the Standards also began to emerge in the winter of 2011 in states that had already adopted them. Republican state legislators in Utah and New Hampshire began to raise objections to the Standards and suggested that the lawmakers wanted a say in their adoption. In Utah, the Senate Majority Caucus adopted a motion asking its House counterparts to join them in sending a letter to the state board of education asking the board to reconsider its decision to adopt the Common Core and instead to reinstate Utah's standards. Senator Chris Butters claimed the Common Core State Standards included "code words for socialism," and stated, "We've got a pig in a poke."[20] In response, Utah's superintendent of public instruction, Larry K. Shumway, issued a statement strongly endorsing the Common Core State Standards. He stated:

> The members of the Utah State Board of Education and the staff at the Utah State Office of Education welcome the senators' interest and encourage their inquiry. After honest investigation, we believe they will come to the same conclusion that the Board has come to: Common core standards will help increase the academic rigor of Utah's public schools and help make students across the nation more academically (and, consequently, economically) competitive with their peers from around the globe.[21]

In New Hampshire, State Representative Ralph Boehm, a Republican, introduced a bill that would require the legislature, along with the state board of education, to approve academic standards. Boehm suggested that the Standards represented an unfunded mandate for local districts. The effort did not succeed, but the proposal, like the Utah proposal, attracted attention from education bloggers across the country.

Meanwhile, for the first time, a local district in Massachusetts sought to reverse that state's decision to adopt the Common Core State Standards. At first, the Tantasqua Regional School Committee tried to get the Massachusetts Association of School Committees to support the board in its fight against the Standards. That request was rebuffed. The board then voted seventeen to zero to ask legislators to introduce a bill overriding the state board of education's vote to adopt the Standards. Representative Todd Smola, a Republican who represents Tantasqua, introduced such a bill in January 2011. As of this writing, the proposal has not gone anywhere. Tantasqua's superintendent, Daniel G. Durgin, said support for the Common Core State Standards was "overwhelming" in Massachusetts, and Glenn Koocher, the executive director of the Massachusetts Association of School Committees, agreed.[22]

In South Dakota, meanwhile, one state legislator hoped to fend off common standards in history, something that did not exist. State Representative Jim Bolin, a former history teacher, argued that that subject was uniquely suited to local interpretation, and he wanted to prevent the state from adopting standards that might be developed outside South Dakota. Although his bill was passed by the state House, the state Senate Education Committee voted it down, arguing that it addressed a nonexistent problem.

These legislative opponents did not roll back their state's initial adoption of the Common Core State Standards, but they would play a role in the next stage of the process: the implementation of the Standards. Now that they had been adopted, states began to take steps to ensure that they become part of policy and classroom practice through changes in assessments, curriculum, and professional development. These changes would in many cases require resources, and legislators hold the purse strings.

6

PUTTING IT TOGETHER

Implementing New Standards

W HEN THE MEMBERS of the Kentucky State Board of Education became the first in the nation to adopt the Common
Core State Standards, they knew that their action was the start, not
the end, of a long process. They knew they had to make sure people
understood the Standards and their implications for instruction,
and they had to provide support so that teachers could integrate
them into their classrooms. Without those actions, the Standards
would become just another document on teachers' bookshelves,
gathering dust.

Working with the Council on Postsecondary Education and the
Educator Professional Standards Board, both of which agreed to
adopt the Standards the same day that the state board did, the board
first took several steps to build public awareness of the Standards. In
August 2010, the board published documents that showed the alignment between Kentucky's previous standards and the Common Core
State Standards. The three organizations also worked with the
Pritchard Committee for Academic Excellence, a prominent civic organization that supports education statewide, to enlist teachers and
parents to communicate about the Standards to their constituents.
The organizations also held informational Webinars and school
meetings, and communicated with the news media to try to get
their message about the new standards across to the public.

The organizations also took steps to align the Standards to the expectations for higher education. If the Standards truly represented the knowledge and skills needed for college and career readiness, then postsecondary institutions needed to embrace them as well. Toward that end, the three organizations held a meeting known as the Unbridled Learning Summit in April 2010 (Kentucky is, after all, the home of Churchill Downs and the Derby) to introduce higher education leaders to the Standards. They then held a series of workshops around the state on the Standards and added higher education representatives to the state department of education's instructional support network, which provides assistance to district administrators throughout Kentucky. Significantly, higher education leaders also developed a course for teacher-preparation institutions that would educate prospective teachers on the Standards and related assessments.

The organizations also began efforts to prepare practicing teachers to work with the Standards. In that effort, they communicated through eight regional educational cooperatives, local networks that included content area specialists , and an additional network led by the Gheens Academy for Curricular Excellence and Instructional Leadership in Louisville, a well-respected institution that provides ongoing training for practicing teachers. The networks identified and developed materials on assessment, instruction, professional development, and school improvement, and made them available through an online professional development portal. They also identified more than eight hundred fifty trained facilitators who would lead professional development at the school level.

And that was not all. The state organizations also began to identify resources to support curriculum development so that teachers would have access to materials on the new standards. The state department of education formed an advisory group to develop a model curriculum framework to show how a year's worth of instruction would lead to mastery of the Standards by the end of the year. The group, which began meeting monthly in September 2010, examined frameworks from U.S. states, such as Connecticut, and from abroad, including Queensland, Australia, and New

Zealand. The department published a Web-based version of the framework in April 2011.

In addition, the department worked with private organizations to strengthen high school coursework. AdvanceKentucky, a science, technology, engineering, and mathematics initiative of the Kentucky Science and Technology Corporation (a nonprofit organization that supports science, technology, and economic development in the state) and Project Lead the Way (a program intended to increase students' interest in pursuing careers in engineering, advanced manufacturing, biomedical sciences, and energy) helped develop science and mathematics courses. And Kentucky Virtual School, a school that provides digital learning for students throughout the state, is helping students, parents, and teachers develop individualized lessons so students learn what they need in order to achieve the Standards.

All of these activities suggest that the adoption of the Common Core State Standards, while hugely significant, pales in scope to what must be done to implement them. Only when teachers make the Standards part of their everyday classroom instruction, when they are prepared to teach them effectively, when the Standards are aligned with assessments that measure them faithfully, and when higher education institutions integrate the Standards into placement decisions and teacher education programs (and parents understand them), will they have a chance of improving student learning.

To add to the challenge, all of these tasks must take place at a time when states are facing the worst budget climate in decades. To make the Standards real and meaningful, states will have to find resources at a time when they are bleeding red ink.

WHAT IMPLEMENTATION MEANS

In an effort to provide a road map for states in implementing the Common Core State Standards, in 2010, Achieve produced a guide for state policy makers that outlines the steps they should consider and the questions they should ask.[1] The guide serves as a rough outline for implementation. The major categories are:

- *"Integrating the Standards into the college- and career-ready agenda."* States need to consider their existing policies that are aimed at preparing students for colleges and careers—including assessments, curriculum, and accountability—and the impact the Standards will have on those policies. States therefore might need to revise assessments and graduation requirements and change or add high school coursework.
- *"Leveraging state budget and funding to support implementation."* States must look at existing resources and other sources of funding to support professional development and curriculum materials.
- *"Comparing state standards to the Common Core State Standards."* States must examine their existing standards to see where gaps exist and where content is no longer relevant.
- *"Aligning instructional materials to the Common Core State Standards."* States must analyze existing materials to determine their match with the Common Core State Standards and adopt new ones that reflect the expectations of the Common Core.
- *"Communications and outreach."* States need to make sure key constituencies are aware of the Common Core State Standards and how they affect them.

A survey of state education department officials conducted in late 2010 by the Center on Education Policy (CEP) provides an early snapshot of state plans to implement the standards. All of the thirty-six states surveyed plan to revise assessments; thirty-three, to revise curriculum guides or materials; thirty-three, to revise professional development programs; thirty-one, to require districts to adopt the Standards; thirty, to revise teacher-evaluation systems to hold educators accountable for student mastery of the Standards; twenty-five, to adopt special measures to ensure the Standards are implemented in the lowest-performing schools; and eighteen, to revise educator-certification policies to align with the Standards.[2]

Few states, however, had plans to change higher-education admissions policies, such as enabling students who meet the Standards to be admitted to college, or to change first-year college courses to reflect the Common Core State Standards.

Many of the more ambitious policies, such as changes in teacher evaluation, were not expected to be implemented before 2013 at the earliest, the survey found. In part, this longer time line reflects the fact that the assessments being developed by the two state consortia are not expected to be fully in place until 2014–2015.

The survey also found that states faced major challenges in implementing the Standards. Specifically, nineteen states cited funding for implementation as a "major" challenge. Significantly, the eleven states that won Race to the Top grants did not see funding as a major challenge.

States also cited changes in teacher-evaluation systems and changes to higher education policies as major challenges. But few saw political opposition to the Standards as a challenge.

STATE IMPLEMENTATION PLANS

States developed various plans to help implement the Standards. They included revising assessments to match the Standards, revising curricula, offering professional development opportunities for teachers, and building awareness of the Standards.

Revising Assessments

As the CEP study indicates, revising state tests is top on the agenda for states implementing the Common Core State Standards. State officials recognize that their assessments need to match the new standards so that the results will indicate progress toward them, and they know that, because of the strong influence of assessments on instruction, changing assessments will encourage teachers to address the content of the Standards. Nearly all states have signed on to join one or both of the consortia that are developing new assessments to measure the Common Core State Standards, but since those assessments are not expected to be in place until 2014–2015, states decided to make a transition between their current assessments and the new ones.

For example, Massachusetts will revise its state assessment, the Massachusetts Comprehensive Assessment System (MCAS), over a three-year period. In 2011–2012, the test will include content from its previous standards that are not included in the Common Core. The following year, the state will drop the outmoded content and instead add content from the Common Core that was not included in previous standards. The goal is to ensure that the assessment is fair to everyone and maintains a trend line over time, according to state officials.

States are also developing assessment resources for teachers to use in classrooms that are tied to the Common Core State Standards. In Missouri, for example, state officials, in collaboration with teachers, are developing an item bank of formative assessments, or measures that teachers can use in the classroom to inform instruction, in order to monitor student progress against the Standards.

Revising Curriculum

Curriculum is also a high implementation priority for states. As noted in chapter 1, the curriculum is often the missing element that makes standards usable in classrooms. Curricula outline what should be taught over the course of a year to enable students to reach the standards and often suggest a sequence of instruction that leads to mastery of the standards.

States implementing the Common Core State Standards are developing curriculum resources in a number of ways. First, many states are putting together curriculum frameworks that outline a course of study for each grade level, based on the Standards. In Ohio, for example, the state board of education in 2011 adopted a model curriculum in English language arts and mathematics that was developed with extensive involvement of the state's educators. Following the adoption of the Common Core State Standards in

2010, the Ohio department of education conducted a series of sixteen regional meetings around the state to consider the curriculum that would support the standards. A group of educators, business leaders, policy makers, and community leaders, known as the International Education Advisory Committee, then drafted a set of model curricula and released them for public comment. The committee then incorporated the comments and revised the documents and submitted them to the state board, which adopted them in March 2011. The state department of education now plans to develop a Web-based tool that will include detailed explanations of the content, learning expectations, and instructional strategies and resources for teachers.

Similarly, the Michigan department of education has created a Teaching for Learning Web site to disseminate curriculum resources and instructional strategies developed by teachers, curriculum specialists, and subject matter experts. The Web site also houses materials from other states and national resources. In addition, in partnership with the Michigan Association of Intermediate School Administrators, the department is also developing model curriculum units, which will include daily lesson plans as well as longer-term units.

Hawaii, meanwhile, sought to identify existing curriculum materials that could support instruction in the Common Core State Standards. The state department asked schools to examine their capacity to implement the Standards using existing resources and conducted an online survey to identify the materials that are currently in use. Beginning in 2013, the state plans to conduct a process to adopt new materials based on the Standards.

Similarly, West Virginia plans to ask teams of teachers to review the Common Core State Standards and state-adopted curriculum materials and identify gaps. Then, a group of teachers will develop a set of electronic resources to fill in the gaps. The teachers will post their resources on a Web-based portal, called Teach 21.

States are also revising standards and curricula in other subjects and grade levels to help ensure that students are ready for colleges and careers. In Maryland, for example, the state department of education is developing a World Languages program in Arabic, Chinese, and Hindi, and working with teachers to create online coursework in those languages. The program will be piloted in kindergarten through grade five.

Additionally, Massachusetts and other states, such as Connecticut, are also extending the Common Core State Standards to the early years. In Connecticut, the state department of education plans to develop early learning standards for children from birth to age five. To guide the development of these standards, the department produced documents that detail the alignment between the Common Core State Standards for kindergarten, Connecticut's prekindergarten standards, and Connecticut's prekindergarten curriculum and assessment frameworks.

Providing Professional Development Opportunities

Professional development is key to standards implementation, and nearly all the states the CEP surveyed plan to educate teachers about the Common Core State Standards and how to teach them effectively. As shown in chapter 4, the Standards in many cases call for quite different instructional expectations than teachers are accustomed to, so enabling teachers to understand what students will be expected to learn and how they can structure classrooms to bring about that learning will be critical to the success of the Standards. Although the Standards documents provide some suggestions for teaching, they do not provide explicit guides for instruction, so helping teachers understand the implications of the Standards is a critical implementation challenge.

Several states are organizing their existing professional development opportunities around the Standards. Oklahoma conducts an annual series of regional conferences; these will focus on helping teachers understand the Common Core State Standards. The state department of education is also creating modules on the Standards and assessments that can be used in workshops, institutes, conferences, and online learning opportunities.

Other states, such as Pennsylvania, are creating new infrastructures for professional development around the Standards. Following a statewide institute in December 2010, the state identified trainers who will educate the staff of intermediate units, agencies that provide support to districts, on the Standards. These staff members will then provide professional development and technical assistance to teachers and administrators at the school level. The Pennsylvania department of education also prepared a document outlining the content of the Common Core State Standards that will be used for professional development providers who work in the state.

States that won Race to the Top grants have been able to use funds to enlist partners from around the country to support professional development around the Standards. Rhode Island, for example, formed a partnership with the Charles A. Dana Center at the University of Texas at Austin to train and certify service providers from private organizations to lead Study of Standards training workshops for teachers. These workshops help teachers understand the Common Core State Standards and prepare them to align curriculum and resources to them.

In New York, another Race to the Top state, the state department of education asked the thirty-seven boards of cooperative educational services (intermediate units) and the five largest school districts to establish teams to work with teachers in implementing the Standards. The teams are expected to hold statewide training sessions as well as quarterly follow-up sessions to prepare teachers to use the Standards effectively.

Building Awareness

In addition to revising policies and practices to align to and support the Common Core State Standards, states are taking steps to build awareness of the Standards and their implications for practice. Colorado, for example, has created a searchable database so that teachers can see the standards for a particular grade or a particular subject over time. Using the database, to take one example, a ninth-grade teacher can see the algebra topics that students should have learned in kindergarten through grade eight, as well as all the mathematics a ninth grader is expected to learn. The database also indicates the previous state standards, so teachers can see what they can retain from previous years' lessons as well as what they need to change.

Colorado is also producing a series of documents aimed at providing a point of view about the standards. These will spell out the kind of teaching and learning that the Standards expect and make clear that the Standards expect more of students. The state will also produce materials that principals and superintendents can use to communicate the expectations to students and parents, and DVDs that show teachers talking about the new Standards, which principals can use in faculty meetings.

TIMING AND PHASING

Many of the state plans for implementing the Common Core State Standards outline detailed time lines to ensure that the implementation can occur at a reasonable pace. Faced with limited resources, states could not conceivably develop all necessary materials and prepare all teachers at once; rather, states proposed to stage the implementation so that they test the materials and expand training over time.

Delaware, one of the first two states to win Race to the Top grants, developed a four-stage plan for implementing the Standards by 2014. In the first phase, which took place in the last half of 2010, the state required core content teachers to complete four online modules and participate in district training to understand the Common Core State Standards. In the second phase, scheduled for 2011 through 2012, teachers in elementary and high schools will begin implementing the Standards by aligning curriculum materials and interim state assessments to them, piloting units of study and lesson plans, and continuing professional development. In the third phase, elementary and high schools will complete the process by implementing aligned curricula and assessments with units of study. In the final phase, the implementation process will be complete in middle schools.

Likewise, Kansas also has a four-stage plan for implementation. A key part of Kansas's plan is the opportunity for teachers, administrators, community members, and other stakeholders to provide feedback along the way. In that way, the state can revise materials and professional development to ensure its effectiveness.

MULTISTATE AND NATIONAL EFFORTS

Unlike previous standards efforts, the Common Core State Standards initiative makes possible multistate and national programs to support implementation. Because states have common standards, they can work together, often with regional and national partners, to develop materials, provide professional development, and create lessons and instructional supports. In fact, this kind of sharing and outreach began to happen even before the final adoption of the Common Core and began to accelerate as the Standards approached their first year in existence.

For example, six states—Florida, Maryland, Kentucky, Texas, Virginia, and West Virginia—have joined with the Southern Regional Education Board to form the Strengthening Statewide College/ Career Readiness Initiative, which is aimed at developing statewide policies and programs to improve students' preparation for post-secondary success. Although the initiative predated the Common Core State Standards—and two of its participants, Texas and Virginia, have not adopted the Standards—the initiative has helped the other four states with their plans for implementation. For example, in Maryland, the initiative is helping the state link educators with representatives from business, higher education, and professional associations to develop higher-level coursework in mathematics and other subjects.

In a statement released in March 2011, a group of seventy-five leading educators, policy makers, and researchers called for "common curriculum content" to accompany the Common Core State Standards, along with "resources to support successfully teaching all students to mastery."[3] The statement, developed by the Albert

Shanker Institute, defined curriculum as "a coherent, sequential set of guidelines in the core academic disciplines, specifying the content knowledge and skills that all students are expected to learn, over time, in a thoughtful progression across the grades. We do not mean performance standards, textbook offerings, daily lesson plans, or rigid pedagogical prescriptions."[4] The statement adds that the curriculum should include sample lessons, examples of student work, and classroom assessments.

The statement did not specify who would develop the common curriculum; instead, it suggests, states could collaborate with one another to develop it, each could develop its own, or "an exemplary curriculum" could be developed by an independent organization. It states that such a curriculum should account for 50 percent to 60 percent of a school's instructional time.

Despite these caveats, the statement sparked a backlash from educators and public officials affiliated with the conservative wing of the political spectrum, who were wary of anything that smacked of a national curriculum and in particular a federal curriculum. In a statement released in May 2011 and signed by a hundred educators and public officials, the group, which was led by commentators who had opposed the Common Core from the outset, stated that they agreed that expectations should be high and the same for all children, but said that they "do not agree that a one-size-fits-all, centrally controlled curriculum for every K–12 subject makes sense for this country or for any other sizable country. Such an approach threatens to close the door on educational innovation, freezing in place an unacceptable status quo and hindering efforts to develop academically rigorous curricula, assessments, and standards that meet the challenges that lie ahead." The group further warned that a common curriculum would undermine local and state control and "transfer control to an elephantine inside-the-Beltway bureaucracy."[5]

But just as dissenting voices about the Standards failed to derail the effort to develop them or the adoption by five-sixths of the states, the manifesto opposing common curriculum did not appear to quell efforts by private organizations to develop materials to support the Common Core State Standards. Indeed, even before the Albert Shanker Institute statement was released, a handful of private organizations were on their way toward developing some form of curriculum aligned with the Common Core State Standards, suggesting that the Standards made possible a new marketplace of materials.

In February 2010, the Core Knowledge Foundation, which supports a network of seven hundred seventy schools that use a common curriculum grounded in content knowledge, announced that it would align its curriculum to the Common Core State Standards and make its classroom materials available free of charge. Foundation officials had criticized an early draft of the Standards, but praised a revised version, which was still undergoing revisions at the time of its announcement about the curriculum.[6]

At about the same time, the Bill & Melinda Gates Foundation, which had been instrumental in supporting the development of the Standards, awarded $19.5 million for the development of instructional tools and formative assessments to support them. With the grants, the graduate school of education at the University of California at Berkeley is building mathematics coursework and assessments aligned with the Common Core State Standards; the Charles A. Dana Center is expanding its pre-algebra 1 summer bridge program into a year-round curriculum that will be available online, free of charge; the Education Trust is developing an open-source literacy course for middle schools; and the Lawrence Hall of Science is creating a version of its elementary curriculum model that fuses science and literacy for middle schools. In addition, the National Center for Research on Evaluation, Standards, and Student Testing (CRESST) at the University of California, Los Angeles, is refining mathematics and literacy assessments, benchmarking them against international assessments, and creating visual representations of learning progressions embedded in the Standards to help teachers understand how students are expected to progress toward college and career readiness over time.[7]

In 2011, the Gates Foundation also awarded $3 million to ASCD, a national organization of school administrators and curriculum specialists, to develop and disseminate a suite of tools to support implementation of the Standards. As part of the three-year effort, ASCD will convene a series of meetings across the country to provide an opportunity for educators to discuss their implementation needs.

In a more controversial step, the Gates Foundation partnered with the Pearson Foundation to develop a set of online courses aligned to the Common Core State Standards. The package will include eleven mathematics courses, one for each grade, kindergarten through grade ten, and thirteen English language arts courses for each grade, kindergarten through grade twelve. Although the foundation plans to make four of the courses available for free, the rest of the courses must be purchased, and some critics questioned whether the arrangement would provide an unfair financial advantage to Pearson's corporate arm, a publishing company. For example, Grover (Russ) Whitehurst of the Brookings Institution said the arrangement raised questions about "who profits from the Common Core."[8]

Other organizations are also developing materials to support the implementation of the Common Core State Standards. The National PTA, for example, in 2011 created the *Parents' Guide to Student Success*, which provides information for parents about the Common Core State Standards. The guides, available in English and Spanish, outline what students are expected to learn at each grade level, what activities parents can do to help their children succeed, ideas for strengthening parents' relationships with their children's teachers, and, at the high school level, tips for planning for college and career.

In addition, in a significant step, the American Council on Education, which administers the General Educational Development (GED) examination for students seeking high school equivalency diplomas, announced in 2011 that it will align that exam with the Common Core State Standards. The council formed a partnership with Pearson, the commercial test publisher, to create a new test, expected to be implemented in 2014, that is intended to indicate the college and career readiness of GED test-takers. Currently, about eight hundred thousand GED tests are taken each year.

HELP FROM THE ASSESSMENT CONSORTIA

As we will see in chapter 7, the U.S. Department of Education in 2010 awarded $330 million to two consortia of states to develop assessments to measure student progress toward the Common Core State Standards. The two assessment consortia, known as the Partnership for Assessment of Readiness for College and Careers (PARCC) and the Smarter Balanced Assessment Consortium, are also planning to create a wealth of tools for teachers. In September 2010, the U.S. Department of Education awarded each consortium $15.8 million to develop and implement materials to support the shift to new state assessments.

The first products under development are model content frameworks intended to guide teachers on the key content in each subject. At a conference in February 2011, Christopher Cross, a former assistant U.S. secretary of education, cautioned that the consortia might be prohibited from developing curricula because they are federally funded; a provision of the statute that established the U.S. Department of Education barred the department from supporting curriculum. However, Michael Cohen, the president of Achieve, which is the managing partner of PARCC, responded that the intention is not to develop curricula but to provide voluntary models of suggested content.

In its proposal, the Smarter Balanced Assessment Consortium (SBAC) said it would create interim or benchmark assessments that teachers could administer during the course of the year to give them ongoing feedback on student learning. The consortium would build assessments around learning progressions, or models of how students develop an understanding of a subject area, so that teachers can identify gaps in student understanding and redesign instruction before students take the accountability tests. In addition, the consortium plans to develop tools and materials and provide opportunities for professional development to help teachers understand the content and performance expectations of the Common Core State Standards, develop model curriculum units, and align curriculum, instruction, and assessment, among other things. "By combining these formative practices and tools with the summative and [interim/benchmark] assessments," the proposal states, "we are developing a system for learning and assessment that will lead to more informed decision making and will result in higher-quality instruction, and thus, higher levels of student achievement."[9]

As part of its supplemental proposal, the consortium said that it would create a digital library of curriculum frameworks, sample instructional units, and formative assessment tools, and that it would involve nearly twenty-eight hundred teachers in identifying or creating these tools. The consortium also plans professional development to help teachers understand the assessment system and how to score test items.

Similarly, PARCC also plans to develop instructional and curriculum tools for teachers. The consortium plans to create the Partnership Resource Center (PRC), an interactive online tool that will include curriculum frameworks and model lessons, as well as test items to use formatively in the classroom. In addition, PARCC will develop an online diagnostic tool that will enable teachers to evaluate the complexity of a particular text. This tool will help teachers identify appropriate materials to enable students to meet the standards for reading increasingly complex texts, a critical component of the Common Core State Standards. The partnership also plans to create an interactive data tool and reports that will help teachers gather and use data on student achievement to support instructional decisions and principals to make decisions about professional development needs.

Under its supplemental grant, PARCC will also create "college-readiness tools," including coursework to help students who are not on track toward college readiness at the end of eleventh grade. Like SBAC, PARCC also plans to create a digital library of curriculum resources and assessment tools.

Both consortia are also taking steps to engage higher education institutions in the implementation of the Standards. The Standards are intended to measure students' readiness for postsecondary education, but they will only have meaning if colleges and universities accept them as measures of readiness. In their proposals, the consortia lined up letters of support from public institutions of higher education in the participating states, which pledged to use them to help place incoming freshman in math and English courses. PARCC received letters of support from 188 institutions; Smarter Balanced received support from 162 institutions. As a first step, PARCC held a meeting with representatives of institutions of higher education in February 2011 to consider the standards that are most important in assessing readiness, as well as the data that would be most useful to postsecondary institutions. Smarter Balanced also added a higher education representative to its governing board. Both consortia are working with higher education leaders to build the assessments and to ensure that the institutions use the high school assessments in placement decisions.

CHALLENGES AHEAD

In the 1990s, the promise of standards-based reform crashed on the shoals of implementation. As noted in chapter 1, standards must be accompanied by high-quality assessments, curriculum, and professional development aligned with the standards; otherwise, the promise of raising expectations for students will go unfulfilled.

The challenge became particularly acute in 2011, when states and districts faced severe budget shortfalls resulting from the economic recession that began in 2008. Few policy makers were looking to take on new initiatives; their goal was to make do with less. Going forward, how can states and national organizations support the implementation of an ambitious set of expectations for student learning?

One way is for states and districts not to view the implementation of the Common Core Standards as a new activity. Rather, they should see it as what they do regularly, only with new tools. States and districts already develop and disseminate curriculum materials and support professional development. Now they will do so around the Common Core State Standards. States can drop some of the materials they have already developed and some of the professional development they provide to focus their efforts on the Standards.

At the same time, the financial crunch will force states and school systems to be smarter about how they spend their money. They should put their emphases on their highest priorities; the Standards should be among them. Governors and chief state school officers have signaled their support for the Standards, and parents and teachers strongly back the idea of educating all students so that they are prepared for college and careers.[10] Putting in place the Standards and systems to ensure that students can meet them ought to be one of the most important things states and districts do over the next few years.

Technology can also help make their efforts more efficient. By putting materials online, states and districts can save money by not printing and distributing reams of paper. Online professional development can reduce costs associated with teacher travel; teachers can also participate at a time that's convenient for them, and districts need not incur the cost of substitutes for teachers taking a day to meet at a central location. To be sure, some face-to-face meetings are valuable, and schools need to carve out time for teachers to meet to plan lessons around the Standards. But schools and school systems can reduce expenses if they think wisely about using technology strategically.

Another concern about implementation relates to the quality of the materials and professional development. Now that the Standards are popular and important, virtually every provider will want to claim that his or her curriculum materials or workshop is aligned to the Standards. Some, but probably not all, will be. Some materials and professional development might not be effective because they will not support what the Standards expect students to learn. As of now, there is no entity that can evaluate the materials against the Standards to determine the strength of the match.

The quality issue is crucial, because, as James Spillane has shown (see chapter 1), people can interpret standards in different ways. Some teachers might regard them as incremental shifts from current practice, while others will see them as a substantial departure.

As chapter 4 shows, the Standards do call for significant changes in practice in many key areas. If the materials and professional development reflect a narrow view, the Standards will not have the impact on student learning they could have.

One significant factor that could help their impact is the new assessments that are being developed. These assessments are expected to be closely aligned to the Standards, and several of the people involved in developing the Standards, such as David Coleman and Jason Zimba, the lead writers for each subject area, are working with the two assessment consortia to ensure that they reflect their intent. The assessments will send a powerful signal to teachers by providing in concrete terms the types of performances students need to demonstrate to meet the Standards. That will help teachers structure classroom work so that students can build the abilities expected of them. In addition, as long as states and districts continue to hold schools accountable for performance on the assessments, the assessments will exert a powerful influence on classroom instruction. Teachers will be sure to model their instruction on what the assessments expect.

In the next chapter, we will look at those expectations and examine the work of the two consortia.

7

ASSESSMENTS

The Next Generation

WHEN U.S. SECRETARY OF EDUCATION Arne Duncan met with Achieve's America Diploma Project leadership team on September 2, 2010, he had some important news to tell them. That morning, the education department awarded a total of $330 million to two groups of states, one managed by Achieve, to develop assessments to measure the Common Core State Standards in English language arts and mathematics.

The announcement was the culmination of a process that began the year before, when Duncan announced that he would award up to $350 million to groups of states to create new testing programs for measuring the common standards. The program was part of Race to the Top, a $4.3 billion initiative to award grants to states to initiate reforms. While the larger program received a good deal of publicity, the smaller assessment grant program could have longer-lasting effects. Duncan noted the importance of the program when he announced the awards:

> Today is a great day! I have looked forward to this day for a long time—and so have America's teachers, parents, students, and school leaders. Today is the day that marks the beginning of the development of a new and much-improved generation of assessments for America's schoolchildren. Today marks the start of Assessments 2.0.

And today marks one more milestone, testifying to the transformational change now taking hold in our nation's schools under the courageous leadership and vision of state and district officials.[1]

Duncan's optimism was not misplaced. The program he was funding indeed had the potential to promote large-scale changes in instruction and learning. This was true for three reasons.

First, while the Common Core State Standards represented a substantial change in expectations for student achievement, research and experience make clear that standards will not have an impact without related assessments. Assessments make the standards concrete; they describe the particular tasks students must accomplish in order to meet the standards. Thus, the assessments Duncan was funding would bring the standards to life.

Second, the proposals by the two state consortia seeking the federal funds called for ambitious changes in the way student performance was measured. In addition to end-of-year tests, which states and school districts had relied on for years as the primary gauge of student achievement, the proposals called for additional measures to be conducted throughout the year, some involving projects that students would work on for several days. While such measures are common in other countries, they represent a substantial breakthrough in U.S. schools.

The proposals also called for a heavy reliance on computer-based testing, which makes possible quick results to students and teachers, and also enables the use of innovative test items, such as simulations and original research. While some states had begun to incorporate online assessments as part of their testing programs, the reliance on technology in the consortia's proposals would constitute a major advance.

Third, the scale of the program made it highly significant. Schools, districts, and states had put in place sophisticated tests over the past twenty years. But forty-four states had signed up to join one or both of the groups of states under the Race to the Top assessment program, as it was known. That meant that the plans the consortia would develop would affect a huge proportion of American schoolchildren.

Before considering the consortia's plans in detail, let's first examine their significance in greater depth by looking at the role of testing in American education.

KNOWING WHAT STUDENTS KNOW

Testing has always loomed large in American schools. Policy makers and taxpayers have long demanded information on how schools are performing, and testing has been considered an objective way of "knowing what students know," as a National Research Council report put it.[2]

The interest in testing is almost as old as American schooling. As early as 1845, Horace Mann, the leader of the common school movement, used a test to help make his case for state support of schooling. In contrast to the oral tests that schools had used, the written test Mann developed with his colleague Samuel Gridley Howe, would "determine, beyond appeal or gainsaying, whether the pupils have been faithfully or competently taught," Mann said.[3]

In recent years, states and districts have dramatically increased the amount of testing in schools, as well as its importance. In the 1970s, in the wake of a report that showed that scores on the Scholastic Aptitude Test (SAT) had declined sharply from 1963 through 1977, thirty-six states adopted laws requiring students to pass tests to demonstrate minimum competency in reading and mathematics. The following decade, after a national commission warned that declining educational performance threatened to put the "nation at risk," states added testing requirements.[4] By the end of the 1980s, forty-seven states had a statewide testing program.

Spurred by the federal government and the standards-based reform movement, states and districts amped up testing again in the 1990s and 2000s. As noted in chapter 2, the 1994 Improving America's Schools Act required states to set standards and develop tests to measure performance against them in at least three grades. No Child Left Behind (NCLB) mandated testing in every grade from third through eighth and once in high school. In addition, half the states adopted tests that students were required to pass in order to graduate from high school.

At the same time, states and districts increasingly placed consequences on test results. These consequences have been most apparent under NCLB; schools that fail to make "adequate yearly progress" toward the goal of proficiency for every student by 2014 are subject to sanctions. These consequences are intended to create incentives for schools to focus on the material that is tested and on students who are struggling, in order to close achievement gaps and raise performance overall.

Research shows that the testing and accountability policies have indeed prompted schools to focus on tests. Teachers and principals adapt their curriculum to what is tested—and pay less attention to what is not tested. And they model instruction on *how* the content is tested.

In some cases, these effects can be beneficial. Studies of writing assessments, for example, found that when states instituted tests that measured student writing, rather than multiple-choice tests of language use, teachers increased the amount of writing they assigned, and student writing performance improved over time.[5]

However, in many cases, the emphasis on tests has been less than healthy and, in some cases, harmful. When tests measure simple factual recall and the use of basic mathematical procedures, teachers spend more of their time teaching those abilities and less on more complex abilities, like research and analysis. They use multiple-choice worksheets in class, rather than ask students to write. And in extreme cases, teachers spend considerable class time drilling students on items like those that appear on the tests, rather than focusing on the concepts students are expected to know.

These practices are understandable, because teachers and principals are under considerable pressure to raise test scores. But they do not improve student learning. Moreover, they skew the picture of student achievement that test scores are supposed to provide. It's as though doctors, faced with a patient with a raging fever, gave the patient massive doses of aspirin. That might lower the fever, at least temporarily, but it does not address the underlying disease.

In an effort to change the incentive structure and encourage better instruction, reformers in the late 1980s and early 1990s developed new types of assessments that attempted to measure more complex abilities by engaging students in extended tasks that asked them to solve problems and write more extensively, rather than simply identify the correct answer from a preselected set of answers. These assessments—known variously as performance assessments or "authentic" assessments—were intended to harness the power of testing to foster improvements in teaching and learning. If teachers are going to teach to tests, the argument went, why not build tests that are worth teaching to?

Some of these efforts represented significant departures from conventional testing practice. Vermont, for example, created a portfolio system that evaluated students' performance on the basis of classroom work they had completed throughout the year; Kentucky also used portfolios in its assessment program. Maryland's assessment included tasks that students performed in groups over several days. Other states included performance-based components in assessments.

As the advocates for these assessments had intended, these performance-based measures often produced positive changes in instruction. Teachers were more likely to engage students in writing and in solving mathematical problems, for example. However, the assessments also proved less reliable as measures of student performance than conventional tests; in Vermont, for example, teachers' ratings of portfolio components varied too widely to enable the portfolios to produce individual student results, at least at first. In addition, the measures attracted critics who contended that they were more subjective and less rigorous than conventional tests.[6]

Moreover, the performance-based assessments also turned out to be more expensive than multiple-choice tests, because they required teachers to grade them. By contrast, multiple-choice tests, which can be scored by machine, are relatively inexpensive. So, after NCLB required states to test students in grades three through eight and once in high school, many states dropped performance-based assessments to save money and avoid the controversies they had engendered.

At the same time, states and districts stepped up the pressure on tests. They developed data systems that enabled teachers and principals to monitor test performance and adjust their instruction and curriculum based on the results. They added interim tests that were essentially mini-versions of end-of-year tests to provide additional data on student achievement throughout the year. And they looked for ways to hold teachers accountable for test results; in 2010, the number of states that required that test results be the preponderant factor in teacher evaluations more than doubled, from four to ten.

COMPREHENSIVE ASSESSMENT SYSTEMS

All this emphasis on tests and test scores drew criticism from a growing chorus of educators and policy makers. Tests were asked to carry weight that no assessment, no matter how sophisticated, could bear. They were expected to serve as reliable guides of student achievement, hold schools accountable for progress, measure teacher performance, and guide instruction. The tests were not designed to serve all of those functions, and they could not.

Worse, it was clear that the NCLB tests were far from the most sophisticated tests. They did not measure the full range of knowledge and skills students were expected to demonstrate, and they did not foster the kind of instruction that leads to high levels of learning.

One critic of state tests was in a prime position to do something about it: President Obama. In remarks to the Hispanic Chamber of Commerce in 2009, he said: "I'm calling on our nation's governors and state education chiefs to develop standards and assessments that don't simply measure whether students can fill in a bubble on a test, but whether they possess 21st century skills like problem-solving and critical thinking and entrepreneurship and creativity."[7]

Taking up the challenge, Arne Duncan announced in June 2009 that he would dedicate up to $350 million from the Race to the Top program, which was made possible by the American Recovery and Reinvestment Act of 2009, to support state efforts to develop new assessments. In announcing the program, Duncan said he wanted to foster a new generation of educational assessments:

> We need tests that measure whether students are mastering complex materials and can apply their knowledge in ways that show that they are ready for college and careers. We need tests that go beyond multiple choice, and we know that these kinds of tests are expensive to develop. It will cost way too much if each state is doing this on its own.[8]

Responding to his call, researchers and education organizations began proposing bold alternatives to conventional testing programs. In an influential paper written in 2010 for the Council of Chief State School Officers (CCSSO), Linda Darling-Hammond, a professor of education at Stanford University and a leading adviser to Obama during the 2008 election, laid out a vision for an assessment *system* that would support high-quality teaching and learning. In her paper, Darling-Hammond proposed a system would include both classroom-based and external measures that would assess the full range of standards students would be expected to meet; it would measure student performance on challenging tasks that ask them to apply their knowledge to solve complex problems; it would involve teachers in the development and scoring of assessments; it would use technology to improve the quality of assessments; and it would provide information that could be used to hold schools accountable for student learning.[9]

Other organizations also called for assessment systems that included a range of measures to serve the various purposes that assessments were being called upon to serve. For example, the National Association of State Boards of Education issued a report urging state policy makers to shift the balance away from heavy reliance on tests for accountability toward an increasing reliance on classroom-based measures that support instruction. Specifically, the report concluded that "states need to create a comprehensive, balanced assessment system that includes both assessment *of* learning (reporting on what's been learned) as well as assessments for learning (providing ongoing feedback to teachers and students as learning progresses."[10]

Similarly, the Alliance for Excellent Education also issued a call for a comprehensive and coherent system. An Alliance publication stated:

> A new assessment system would redesign the summative tests used for accountability purposes and embed them in a comprehensive and coherent system in which curriculum, instruction, and assessment are intertwined. Think of the system as a wheel—at the hub are the common core standards, and the spokes include summative assessments, formative assessments, curriculum tasks, instructional tools, and professional development. In such a system, assessments are not separate and apart from classroom instruction, they are integral to it. All forms of assessment provide an ongoing information loop to teachers, school leaders, parents, policymakers, and the public.[11]

Even testing companies joined the call for dramatically new assessments. In a joint paper submitted to the U.S. Department of Education, researchers from the College Board, the Educational Testing Service (ETS), and Pearson, a leading test publisher, proposed an integrated system that would include end-of-year tests that measure what students have learned and classroom-based interim assessments that support instruction, both linked to a common framework. They also called for including measures that students would take during the course of the school year and using computer technology to score assessments rapidly in developing new types of test questions. The paper concluded:

> We believe that we can create a summative assessment system that uses innovative exercise types and computer adaptive delivery to measure depth of student understanding and track student growth. The system can be designed in ways that allow it to work hand-in-hand with formative assessment elements to produce instructionally actionable data. We can provide solid data on common-core standards

while giving states a chance to add their own augmentations. We can do this in a way that is operationally and economically feasible.[12]

This growing consensus for a new type of assessment system reflected a number of factors. First, there was a growing dissatisfaction with the current system of tests, as President Obama and Secretary Duncan made clear. They and others knew that the current system did not measure the full range of knowledge and skills that students need to know and be able to do, and that they created some harmful side effects on instruction.

Second, there was a greater understanding that nations that perform well on international comparisons employed very different assessment systems, and that their practices showed that new approaches were not only feasible, but that they produced better results. One of the most influential students of international practices was Darling-Hammond, who drew on her examination of testing policies in Europe and Asia in her report for CCSSO. She noted that high-scoring nations like Australia, Hong Kong, and Singapore have sophisticated assessment systems that include classroom-based tasks as well as tests administered by states and national governments and that involve teachers extensively in the development and scoring of assessment tasks. These nations test students less frequently than the United States does, but Darling-Hammond's paper suggests that the principles could be adapted to the more extensive testing required by state and federal law in this country.

The third reason for the newfound boldness in the vision for new assessment systems was advances in technology, which made possible new forms of testing that would have been difficult if not impossible a decade ago. In contrast to the 1990s, when states attempted to create performance-based assessments using pencil and paper and handheld materials, new technologies enabled test developers to create performance tasks that engage students in complex problem solving and could measure their skills much more efficiently. As the ETS–College Board–Pearson paper put it: "Technology allows for the use of a range of forward-looking exercise types, including item types that ask students to engage with digital content and formats, and bring to bear skills that wouldn't (and couldn't) be invoked on a paper test."[13]

THE RACE IS ON

After holding ten hearings and receiving testimony from forty-two experts and nearly a thousand comments from members of the public, the U.S. Department of Education officially launched its $350 million assessment competition in April 2010. It called for proposals from consortia of states to develop comprehensive assessment systems that would measure the Common Core State Standards in English language arts and mathematics in grades three through eight and at least once in high school. And the department called for proposals for a second competition to develop high school end-of-course examinations, to increase the number of students in challenging high school courses.

Specifically, the competition for comprehensive assessment systems, which would provide up to $160 million each to as many as two state consortia, specified that groups of no less than fifteen states could apply for grants. They would have to develop assessments that measured the full range of standards for college and career readiness and that elicited "complex student demonstrations or applications of knowledge and skills where appropriate." In addition, the notice stated that the assessments "must produce data (including student achievement data and student growth data) that can be used to inform (a) determinations of school effectiveness; (b) determinations of individual principal and teacher effectiveness for purposes of evaluation; (c) determinations of principal and teacher professional development and support needs; and (d) teaching, learning, and program improvement."[14] That is, the assessments would not only produce information on how students performed, but also show how students improved over time, in order to help measure teacher and school leader effectiveness and direct resources to where they were needed.

The competition for high school assessments, which would provide up to $30 million for one consortium, specified that consortia of at least five states could apply for grants to develop new assessments for multiple high school courses that have common expectations for rigor. The competition provided additional points for programs that promoted coursework in science, technology, engineering, and mathematics (STEM) and in career and technical education.

In an elaborate mating ritual—more akin to speed dating because states had only two months to submit proposals—states quickly formed partnerships to create assessment consortia. At one time, as many as seven consortia had formed. One, led by Oregon, which had pioneered the use of computer-adaptive assessments, focused on that aspect; one intended to build classroom-based formative assessments, and one focused solely on high school assessments. Other groups of states, along with testing organizations like the College Board and ACT, also explored the high school proposal.

In the end, most of the consortia merged. Two groups of states, one calling itself the Smarter Balanced Assessment Consortium (SBAC) and one calling itself the Partnership for Assessment of Readiness for College and Careers (PARCC), bid on the comprehensive assessment grant. We will examine their proposals in the next section.

A third partnership, allied with the National Center on Education and the Economy, a Washington-based education organization that had cited international practices in calling for a dramatic restructuring of the U.S. education system, bid on the high school grant. That consortium, known as the State Consortium on Board Examination Systems (SCOBES), consisted of twelve states, led by Kentucky. The group did not intend to create an assessment. Rather, it intended to use existing examination systems like the International Baccalaureate—including curricula and course syllabi—and align them to the Common Core State Standards. The consortium would make available at least three examinations from which states could choose and would set a passing score on the exams that is equivalent to the entrance requirement for state universities. Students could take the courses at any time, but usually in tenth grade, and if they passed the exams, they could enter a state college or university. Or, if they chose to do so, they could stay in high school and take advanced coursework or a career and technical path.

In theory, all three of the consortia could have won. However, the peer reviewers who examined the proposals did not rate SCOBES high enough to earn an award. Several of the reviewers suggested in their comments that the proposal lacked sufficient detail to explain how the group would carry out its plans and whether it would address the needs of all students, including those who were far behind grade level.

Duncan announced the awards to the Smarter Balanced and PARCC consortia at the Achieve leadership meeting in September 2010. The PARCC consortium received $170 million; Smarter Balanced received $160 million. The department subsequently awarded the two groups $15.8 million each to assist in the implementation of their plans, including the development of instructional tools for teachers. It also created two separate competitions for consortia of states to develop additional new assessments, one for alternate evaluations for students with disabilities who cannot participate in regular assessments, and one for English language proficiency assessments for English language learners.

SMARTER BALANCED AND PARCC

As of early 2011, the Smarter Balanced consortium consisted of thirty states, and PARCC consisted of twenty-five states. The total adds up to more than fifty (actually more than fifty-one, because the District of Columbia is part of PARCC), because states could join the consortia at two levels. Governing states, which set policy for the groups, had to commit to one or the other from the outset. But another group of states could join as "advisory" states (in Smarter Balanced) or "participating" states (in PARCC); these could contribute to the development but did not have to commit to joining one or the other (or neither) until the consortia were ready to field-test their assessments. Ten states served as advisory or participating states in both consortia; these were known colloquially as "promiscuous" states. Five states—Alaska, Minnesota, Nebraska, Texas, and Virginia—did not join either consortium (see box 7.1).

BOX 7.1
STATES IN CONSORTIA

Smarter Balanced Assessment Consortium (SBAC) States
(as of June 29, 2011)

Alabama	Maine*	Pennsylvania
California*	Michigan*	South Carolina
Colorado	Missouri*	South Dakota
Connecticut*	Montana*	Utah*
Delaware	Nevada*	Vermont*
Hawaii*	New Hampshire*	Washington*
Idaho*	North Carolina*	Wisconsin*
Iowa*	North Dakota	Wyoming
Kansas*	Ohio	West Virginia*
Kentucky	Oregon*	

*Governing State

Source: Smarter Balanced Assessment Consortium, http://www.k12.wa.us/SMARTER/

Partnership for Assessment of Readiness for College and Careers (PARCC) States
(as of July 8, 2011)

Alabama	Illinois*	New York*
Arizona*	Indiana*	North Dakota
Arkansas*	Kentucky	Ohio
Colorado	Louisiana*	Oklahoma*
Delaware	Maryland*	Pennsylvania
District of Columbia	Massachusetts*	Rhode Island*
Florida*	Mississippi	South Carolina
Georgia*	New Jersey*	Tennessee*

*Governing board state.

Source: Partnership for Assessment of Readiness for College and Careers, http://www.parcconline.org/about-parcc.

Under the terms of the agreement, states would have to adopt the Common Core State Standards by the end of 2011 in order to participate, and nearly all had done so by the end of 2010. The consortia were expected to field-test their assessments in 2013–2014 and put them in place in 2014–2015.

The plans of the two groups were similar, but included some important differences. Smarter Balanced was heavily influenced by the work of Darling-Hammond, who served as the consortium's senior research adviser. As noted earlier, Darling-Hammond had published a report calling for a comprehensive assessment system that would support instruction and learning, and the consortium's plan followed many of those recommendations. Specifically, its plan called for a summative assessment that would include a range of test item formats, including multiple-choice questions, open-ended questions, and "technology enhanced" questions—those that ask students to manipulate their responses via computer, such as moving a line segment to show what a 35-degree angle looks like. This range of formats would enable the assessment to measure the full range of the Common Core State Standards. The summative assessment would be administered in the last twelve weeks of the school year. In addition, the assessment would include an extended "performance event," such as a task that asks students to analyze a series of texts and to write an essay on the same theme. The performance events are intended to allow students to demonstrate their ability to apply their knowledge across multiple standards. In grades three through eight, students would engage in two performance events each year in English language arts and mathematics. In high school, students would take part in a total of six performance events by grade eleven. Each performance event would take one to two class periods to complete. (Box 7.2 shows an example of the kinds of performance events the assessment might include.)

In addition to the summative assessment, the plan also called for interim assessments that would be optional for schools. Teachers could build these assessments from an item bank the consortium would develop; all of the items would be aligned to the Common Core State Standards, and teachers could administer them anytime

---

BOX 7.2

SAMPLE TECHNOLOGY-ENHANCED ITEM

Fifteen students watched a movie and rated the movie on a scale of 1 (very bad movie) to 20 (very good movie). Their ratings are shown in the table.

a. Using the data in the table, complete the box-and-whisker plot by adding the upper quartile, the lower quartile, and the median. A box will be formed with the three points indicated. You will be able to adjust the box once created if needed.

Movie Ratings

Student	Rating	Student	Rating	Student	Rating
Andy	14	Jasper	11	Rose	13
Bee	8	Jenn	12	Sam	4
Cory	5	Katie	13	Sophie	7
Doug	8	Martin	9	Thomas	12
Jamal	5	Pat	11	Young	9

Click on the line to add the upper quartile, lower quartile, and median.

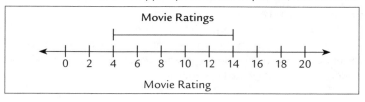

(continued)

---

during the school year. They would be designed according to learning progressions, or the typical pathways of student learning in a subject area (see chapter 4), so that teachers could see where students are on the pathway toward the end-of-year standards. The consortium would also develop a range of formative assessment tools, which would enable teachers to gauge their students' learning during the course of the year and assist them in tailoring their instruction to support students. These assessments would not be used for accountability purposes.

FIGURE 7.2

SAMPLE TECHNOLOGY-ENHANCED ITEM *(continued)*

---

b. The teacher gave the movie a rating of 8. The teacher's rating was added to the ratings of the 15 students. Explain how the addition of the teacher's rating will affect the:

- minimum
- maximum
- upper quartile
- lower quartile
- median

Source: Smarter Balanced Assessment Consortium, Race to the Top Assessment Program: Application for New Grants: Comprehensive Assessment System, CFDA Number 84.395B, Submitted by Washington State on Behalf of the Smarter Balanced Assessment Consortium (Olympia, WA: Washington State Department of Public Instruction, June 2010). Reprinted by permission.

All of the assessments in the Smarter Balanced consortium would be administered on computer, and they would be computer-adaptive. That is, the computer would adjust the items depending on how well the students performed on earlier items. If students did well, they would receive more difficult items; if they did poorly, they would receive easier ones. Computer-adaptive assessments are better able to measure high performance and low performance efficiently than traditional tests, which include a range of items from easy to difficult.

The Smarter Balanced consortium plans to issue annual reports that show how each student performed on the standardized and performance assessments, and that indicate whether students are ready for colleges and careers (in high school) or on track toward college and career readiness (in earlier grades). The reports will also include a measure of annual growth, rather than simply indicating whether students are proficient or not. The interim and benchmark assessments will be scored on the same scale as the summative assessments so that teachers will know if students are on track toward proficiency during the course of the year.

The PARCC proposal also called for an end-of-year summative assessment that would include an array of different item types, all aligned to the Common Core State Standards. The original proposal also called for "through-course" assessments (as opposed to end-of-course assessments) that would be administered at designated periods every twelve weeks during the year, much like end-of unit tests. The idea was that the assessment would measure students' knowledge and skills closer to when instruction takes place. The third through-course assessment would involve an extended performance task. In English language arts, for example, students would have time to read research materials and prepare an extended essay. They would then present their findings to the class; this presentation would be scored on a common rubric according to the Common Core State Standards for speaking and listening. Scores on the three through-course assessments would be combined with those on the end-of-year assessments to provide information for accountability purposes. The speaking-and-listening assessment would not count for accountability. The consortium subsequently revised its proposal to make the through-course components optional, while maintaining the plan for a performance task. (Figure 7.3 shows an example of a performance task in mathematics that was included in the PARCC proposal.)

The results would be reported against benchmarks for college and career readiness and, at the high school level, would indicate whether a student "needs improvement," is "approaching ready," is "ready," or is "advanced." In earlier grades, the reports would indicate whether a student "needs improvement," is "nearly on track," "on track," or "advanced." The reports would also show growth over time.

Like the Smarter Balanced assessments, the PARCC assessments would be administered on computer, at least in grades six and

FIGURE 7.3

MATH PERFORMANCE ITEM: RADIO FREQUENCIES

The Federal Communications Commission (FCC) needs to assign radio frequencies to seven new radio stations located on the grid in the accompanying figure. Such assignments are based on several considerations including the possibility of creating interference by assigning the same frequency to stations that are too close together. In this simplified situation it is assumed that broadcasts from two stations located within 200 miles of each other will create interference if they broadcast on the same frequency, whereas stations more than 200 miles apart can use the same frequency to broadcast without causing interference with each other. The FCC wants to determine the smallest number of frequencies that can be assigned to the six stations without creating interference.

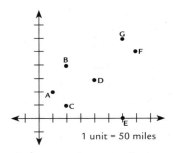

1 unit = 50 miles

- Student 1 began thinking about the problem by drawing a circle of radius 200 miles centered on each radio station.

- Student 2 began thinking about the problem by drawing line segments to connect pairs of radio station whenever the two radio stations are within 200 miles of one another.

- Student 3 began thinking about the problem by drawing line segments to connect pairs of radio station whenever the two radio stations are more than 200 miles from one another.

Which approach seems most promising to you? Use this approach to determine the smallest number of frequencies that can be assigned to the six stations without creating interference. Justify your final answer.

Source: Source: Partnership for Assessment of Readiness for Colleges and Careers, Race to the Top Assessment Competition Proposal Appendix. Adapted from National Council of Teachers of Mathematics, *Focus in High School Mathenatics: Reasoning and Sense Making*, ©2009, National Council of Teachers of Mathematics, reprinted with permission.

above. The consortium plans to conduct research to determine the effects of administering computer-based tests to younger students, who might lack keyboarding skills. The PARCC assessments would not be computer-adaptive.

PARCC also plans to develop formative assessments and other instructional tools, such as curriculum maps to help teachers design a course that would teach the standards for the year. And both consortia plan to develop a Web-based portal that would provide assessment results and information for students, parents, policy makers, and the general public.

Although the two consortia are in some ways competitors, they are working closely together. They hold regular joint conference calls and coordinate their schedules so that they can meet together with other groups. They plan to conduct some of their research jointly, because they have similar questions and working together to solve their problems would be more efficient. They are issuing their first requests for proposals together for a tool states could use to determine their readiness to implement online assessments.

The consortia also are considering creating a Web portal together, so that users can see the results from both assessments. And they are looking into ways their results can be placed on a similar scale, so that the results can be compared across states and across consortia.

Significantly, both of the consortia are working closely with the architects of the Common Core State Standards as they develop test blueprints and items. This type of cooperation is almost unprecedented in test making; test development is usually separate from standards writing. Yet it is absolutely critical to ensure that the tests faithfully measure what the Standards expect. In that way, assessment results will be more likely to reflect what the Standards consider college and career readiness.

CHALLENGES AHEAD

Achieving the ambitious goals that the two consortia have set will be no easy task. They are entering uncharted territory. How they navigate that terrain will determine whether they produce a new generation of assessments that do what NCLB-era tests did not or whether they will create just another set of tests.

One of the biggest challenges the consortia face is simply managing themselves. States have very little experience working together on such a large-scale and high-profile venture, in education or in any other field. States have different laws, regulations, and traditions, and getting them to agree on almost every operational detail in order to move forward is no small task.

One precedent for this step is the New England Common Assessment Program (NECAP), a partnership involving New Hampshire, Rhode Island, Vermont, and eventually Maine. After the passage of NCLB, these small states recognized that they lacked the resources to build high-quality tests for grades three through eight and one for high school, so they decided to pool their resources to build a common instrument that would serve all four states.

This effort resulted in what many consider a high-quality test and saved the states money, but leaders of the effort acknowledge that the members of the partnership had several advantages that made it successful. For example, the states are small and close together, so the participants could meet frequently. In addition, they came into the partnership with a number of shared values; two of the states had already been using the same assessment, the New Standards Reference Examination.[15]

Despite these advantages, the partners also had to meet a number of challenges to make the partnership work effectively. For example, the states had different laws and policies regarding assessments that they needed to work out. Most significantly, the Maine legislature had to approve a change in the timing of the state test from the spring to the fall, when NECAP would be administered; that was a major reason Maine entered the partnership several years after the other states. And even after it entered, Maine chose to use a different test for high schools; Maine administers the SAT to all students in eleventh grade.

PARCC and Smarter Balanced are working with organizations that have experience developing and administering assessments with groups of states. PARCC's managing partner is Achieve, which, through its America Diploma Project network, has developed an algebra 2 test in fifteen states and an algebra 1 test in five states. WestEd, the managing partner for Smarter Balanced, has developed a science test that is used in a number of districts and states, and has developed statewide assessments in eight states and provided technical assistance to half the states.

The two consortia also face some thorny political decisions that will affect the impact of the Common Core State Standards and the power of the assessments in helping to drive change. One key issue will be setting performance standards. Although the states that have signed on to the Standards have agreed on the content students should know, they have yet to determine the level of knowledge and skills students need to demonstrate—how good is good enough? As we have seen, the variations in performance standards used to generate "proficiency" scores and the relatively low standards set in some states were driving forces behind the development of the Common Core State Standards. Without agreement on challenging performance standards, the Common Core effort could be undermined.

Even though the content standards are high, performance standards can be set low if the individuals who set the standards determine that students do not need to demonstrate a solid mastery of the content standards in order to be successful. Gregory J. Cizek, a professor of education and measurement at the University of North Carolina at Chapel Hill, provides an example of low performance standards on challenging material: suppose students are asked to take a test of pediatric ophthalmology delivered in Iraqi Arabic. For most students, that would be very difficult. But suppose the performance standard were set so that students only had to answer four out of twenty items correctly in order to be considered "proficient"— or "college and career ready." Would that standard represent competency in challenging content?[16]

The challenge of maintaining high standards is even greater for the consortia, because all of the states within each consortium are expected to set a common performance standard. But finding an appropriate level among states with very different current levels of performance will be difficult. If the standard is set too low, residents of Massachusetts might balk, because their current standards are high and they signed on to the Common Core State Standards with the assurance that they would not lower their standards. But if the standard is set at a high level, even close to that of Massachusetts, will a state like Mississippi, where students currently perform far less well, agree? Mississippi's results will look quite low, at least at first.

If that political challenge were not enough, the consortia have also pledged to find a way to make the results on both of their assessments comparable, so that residents in Washington State, the leader of Smarter Balanced, could see how their results stack up against those of Florida, the leader of PARCC. Yet comparing the results from different tests is not always feasible. In some cases, when tests measure roughly the same content and are administered in similar ways, these kinds of comparisons are possible and can produce some useful information. For example, the College Board and ACT have for years established tables that show how a student who earned, say, a 600 on the SAT would have performed on the ACT.

But in many other circumstances, these types of comparisons are difficult to achieve. A 1999 report from a committee of the National Research Council, which examined whether it would be feasible to link the results from state tests to show performance on a common scale, as an alternative to a proposed national test, cast cold water on the proposition. The committee concluded:

> Under limited conditions it may be possible to calculate a linkage between two tests, but multiple factors affect the validity of inferences drawn from the linked scores. These factors include the content, format, and margins of error of the tests; the intended and actual uses of the tests; and the consequences attached to the results of the tests. When tests differ on any of these factors, some limited interpretations of the linked results may be defensible while others would not.[17]

The two consortia's assessments might meet those conditions, because the content, uses, and consequences associated with the tests are expected to be similar. But states will need to be careful about the inferences they draw from the results.

The two consortia also face some other technical challenges if they want to realize their ambitious goals. Many of their plans test the current limits of assessment technology. For example, the consortia plan to use artificial intelligence extensively to score student responses to open-ended assessment items. This technology would reduce costs, since it would not require states to bring together scorers to evaluate the responses. And it would provide results to students, parents, and schools much more quickly than relying on human scoring.

However, while the technology of automated scoring has advanced in recent years, there are still some problems associated with it. Computer-scoring systems generally work by examining human-scored essays and determine criteria that would predict the human scores. But the criteria are not always ones that human scorers would use; for example, the length of an essay might be associated with a score, but it is not necessarily the main factor that a human would have used to rate an essay.[18]

In addition, there is an educational value in human scoring that might be lost if computers grade all tests. Teachers often say that scoring examinations is good professional development because it provides them with a clear sense of the standards students are expected to meet and the kind of student work that exemplifies the standards. They also gain value from working with fellow teachers during scoring sessions. One way the consortia could retain this value is by allowing some forms of teacher scoring as a check on the computer ratings.

Another technical issue involves the use of multiple assessments as part of the accountability ratings. As noted earlier, both consortia plan to include a performance event as well as an end-of-year summative assessment and use the results from both to produce scores.

The use of these measures raises a number of challenges. For example, the consortia will need to develop rules for aggregating the results from the different assessments to produce a final score. One way to do that would be simply to add them up and produce a result. But that method might not be sound. If students are expected to learn more over the course of the year, the earlier assessments should count less than the later ones. But assigning weights should also take into account the content on the assessments: if a skill assessed on a later assessment matters less than one assessed on an earlier through-course assessment, the skill that is most important should assume greater weight. To take an example, a winter assessment might measure students' ability to write an essay based on evidence. The spring assessment might measure apostrophe rules. Clearly, writing ability is more important for career and college readiness than knowledge of apostrophe rules and should count more toward the student's score, even though the apostrophe test came later in the year.[19]

Another issue involves what to do with the results from the midyear assessments. Ideally, schools would want to report those results to give students, parents, and teachers an idea of how students are performing during the year, rather than waiting until the end of the year. But if the midyear assessments include fewer items than an end-of-year test and if they rely heavily on performance tasks, as they are expected to, the assessments might not be as reliable as they would be for more extensive tests. The results might be erroneous.[20]

Moreover, the midyear results might provide misleading estimates for how a student will perform at the end of the year. Depending on the content that is tested—whether it measures something that was just taught or something that a student learned earlier—the prediction might understate or overstate an actual score.[21]

In addition to the technical challenges, the states in the two consortia also face the problem of implementing their assessments once they are developed. The funds the U.S. Department of Education provided, while substantial, were only for the *development* of a new assessment. States must administer the assessments year after year. And the consortia must continually build new test items and refine their assessments, particularly since both plan to release a large number of previously used items for teachers to use in the classroom.

The number of test items required is substantial. Smarter Balanced, for example, will need to develop between *80,000 and 100,000* items, because it is using a computer-adaptive test, in which different students essentially take different tests. Creating a test item requires initial development, as well as field-testing to ensure that students can understand the directions and that it measures what it is expected to measure. By one estimate, developing just one multiple-choice item costs between $30 and $100.[22]

A study of the cost of high-quality assessments found that those that use open-ended and performance tasks can cost three times as much as the multiple-choice tests, primarily because of the cost of scoring. However, the study found that these costs could be reduced if states develop tests jointly as a consortium, and if they use technology for scoring. The total costs could end up being less than what a typical state pays for assessments—about $10 per pupil.[23] However, states vary in the amount they currently pay for assessments, and these costs could represent an increase. At a time when state budgets are shrinking, these additional costs might seem like an extravagance.

Yet why should $10 per pupil—or even $20 per pupil—be out of reach? Districts currently spend, on average, more than $10,000 per pupil on elementary and secondary education. Why wouldn't schools spend one-tenth of 1 percent of that total—even two or three tenths of 1 percent—to provide better information on what students know and are able to do? If states are serious about the Common Core State Standards, and forty-three states and the District of Columbia have committed to them by adopting them, then the surest way they can make the Standards real is by putting in place assessments that truly measure expectations.

Whether states choose to go this way will help determine whether the Common Core State Standards can fulfill their potential and transform American education.

8

PROMISE AND CHALLENGES

The Future of the Common Core State Standards

I N A WIDELY READ PAPER he wrote more than a decade ago, Richard F. Elmore argued that the problem with education reform is not the resistance to change or the failure of schools to change, but rather the inability to produce meaningful improvements at scale. Schools are constantly changing, Elmore noted; they are implementing new curricula, devising new schedules, instituting new forms of governance and decision making, and making a host of other modifications. But these changes have not led to improvement because they have not addressed what he called the "core of schooling"—how teachers' ideas about knowledge and learning are reflected in teaching and class work. Reforms that address the core have been implemented on a small scale, but larger-scale reforms made possible by policy changes have not affected the core. In fact, Elmore argued, "the closer an innovation gets to the core of schooling, the less likely it is that will influence teaching and learning on a large scale."[1]

The Common Core State Standards have the potential to upend Elmore's postulate. The Standards could become the innovation that affects teaching and learning on a large scale. The reasons for optimism about the potential of the Standards were outlined in chapter 1. To recount:

- The Standards are clear and can provide guidance to classroom teachers about the kinds of learning students are expected to demonstrate.
- The assessments that are under development are closely tied to the Standards and will create a strong incentive as well as a powerful guide to teachers to teach to the Standards.
- The fact that nearly all the states have adopted the Standards gives national organizations, private firms, and colleges and universities the incentive to develop or revamp curriculum materials, professional development, and teacher preparation around the Standards.

Of course, these standards are only in English language arts and mathematics. But there is an effort under way to develop common standards in science as well. The National Research Council is developing a framework for common standards in that subject area, and Achieve will be pulling together a group of scientists and science educators to draft a set of standards based on that framework. That effort is expected to be completed in 2012, and states will decide whether to adopt those standards. Common standards in other academic areas might also be on the way.

What would a world with common standards look like, and what will it take to get there? This chapter examines those questions.

CLASSROOM PRACTICE

Let's begin with Elmore's core of schooling—teaching and learning in the classroom. Currently, there is wide variation in what teachers teach—even in the same school. In fact, the differences in instructional practices are greater within schools than between schools, even in schools that had implemented fairly prescriptive reform models. A study of teachers in 112 schools found that fifth-grade teachers spent anywhere from 52 days a year to 140 on reading comprehension.[2]

The Common Core State Standards will not eliminate this variability. No one would want to eliminate it altogether; teachers need the flexibility to use their judgment and plan lessons according to their students' needs. And the Common Core State Standards spell out the ends that teachers should seek; they do not specify the steps teachers should take during the course of the year to get there. There are many paths teachers can take to ensure that students meet the Standards, and schools are free to adopt pathways that are appropriate for their students.

However, the Common Core State Standards provide a common vocabulary for teachers that will enable them to work together to develop and plan lessons. Marshall Smith and Jennifer O'Day envisioned this benefit when they laid out the case for standards (or curriculum frameworks) in their seminal article on systemic school reform. As they pointed out, the ability to have a professional dialogue about instruction based on common standards would truly empower teachers.[3]

This dialogue happens in other countries that have common standards. In Japan, for example, teachers regularly engage in "lesson study," during which they work together to develop lessons based on the common standards, try them out, examine the data, and refine them.[4]

To be sure, teachers now can do this within states, since all states have adopted standards. And many do, although teachers in the United States have far less time than teachers in other countries to collaborate and plan lessons jointly. But the Common Core opens up the conversation across states. The availability of Internet communications and Web-based tools make this kind of collaboration possible and easy. For example, the Council of Chief State School Officers has developed a Web-based portal known as EdSteps, on which teachers can post lessons, comment on how they worked in practice, and communicate with peers from across the country who are interested in trying them in their classrooms. More efforts like this will likely spring up once the Common Core State Standards are fully implemented. Thus, the ability of teachers to innovate and try new approaches will be enhanced, not restricted, by the Standards.

In addition, the state consortia that are developing assessments to measure the Common Core State Standards are also developing a wealth of resources for teachers. Both consortia plan to create banks of test items and tasks that teachers can use in the classroom to measure students' performance against the Standards. These tasks can provide formative information that can enable teachers to gauge their students' learning in real time and adjust instruction accordingly.

The consortia are also developing model content frameworks that will help schools and teachers lay out a plan for the year to enable students to meet the standards, as well as model lessons that are tied to the frameworks and the standards. What will these lessons be? What will teachers teach? The Standards offer some clues.

Students will read increasingly complex texts in all subject areas. The current practices in which students read less and less challenging texts or have texts read to them would go away, because students will have to demonstrate their ability to comprehend the kind of material they will confront in college and the workplace. Students will encounter these texts in all their classes, not just English language arts. They will be asked frequently to demonstrate their understanding of these texts by using evidence from the materials to make claims or respond to questions.

Students will also do a lot of writing that asks them to draw on evidence to make logical and reasoned arguments. Opinions will not be enough; students will need to be able to cite facts to back up their arguments. Increasingly, they will need to show a command of the conventions of English and skill in using language to convey ideas and persuade readers.

In mathematics, students in the early grades will develop a strong foundation in arithmetic that will prepare them for algebra and other higher-level mathematics classes. In middle school, they will understand distributions, a key concept in statistics, and prepare to take algebra. And in high school, they will be able to use their knowledge to model mathematics and solve problems in real-world situations.

But all of these activities need not take place in the classroom; in fact, they probably won't. Increasingly, students will be engaging in digital learning, working online to gain access to high-quality content, and using technology for simulations and other experiences unavailable in classrooms. In addition, digital learning affords opportunities for students to interact with peers from across the street, across the country, and indeed across the globe to collaborate on projects, share ideas, and offer feedback. Students can also have access to experts who can supplement the materials they are reading in the classroom.

More typically, students will combine their digital learning with in-class experiences. In that way, the Web can offer top-notch content while enabling teachers in the classroom to do what they do best: work with individual students to guide them when they are struggling, offer suggestions, and provide assistance.

Common Core State Standards make the online resources more feasible than ever before. Since nearly every state has the same standards, the experts and teaching resources need not be confined to a single state. Students can gain access to resources anywhere, since these resources will be useful almost everywhere.

Unfortunately, current evidence suggests that these tools are vitally necessary, because students are a long way from where the Standards expect them to be. A study by ACT, which examined how students in states where the college-admissions test is mandatory for all students performed against the Standards (as measured by ACT college-ready benchmarks), found that only 38 percent of eleventh graders met the Standard in reading; 51 percent, in writing; and 53 percent, in language. The results were lower in mathematics: 34 percent met the Standard in number and quantity; 35 percent, in algebra; 42 percent, in functions; 33 percent, in geometry; and 37 percent, in statistics and probability. Moreover, there were large gaps in performance between white students and African Americans and Hispanics.[5]

TEACHER EDUCATION

To ensure that students are capable of developing the abilities the Standards expect them to master, teachers need to be capable of teaching the knowledge and skills spelled out in the Standards and of organizing classrooms and lessons so that students can learn what they need. Toward that end, teacher preparation programs will align themselves to the Standards. That means that institutions that prepare teachers—institutions of higher education and alternative providers—will need to give them opportunities to engage students in the kinds of challenging activities they will be expected to engage them in as teachers, and will be judged on whether they can improve student learning through those opportunities.

Such changes are already under way. The Council of Chief State School Officers in 2011 has developed model standards for teachers that are aligned with the Common Core State Standards. These standards emphasize the importance of critical thinking and communication, key elements in the Common Core, and stress the need for teachers to teach literacy across the curriculum.[6] The teaching standards, if adopted by states, are intended to influence or become the basis for licensure standards and standards for teacher evaluation.

Nearly half the states also have agreed to take part in a pilot effort to implement a performance assessment for prospective teachers. This assessment will measure whether candidates for teacher licensure can demonstrate, in real classroom settings, the knowledge and skills they will need to demonstrate as practicing teachers—before they earn a license. Such teachers will also have to show that they understand what they are doing by reflecting on their work and showing evidence of student progress.[7]

PROFESSIONAL DEVELOPMENT

Strengthening the preparation of beginning teachers is not enough. There are more than three million teachers currently practicing in American schools, and they were not prepared for a world in which the Common Core State Standards set expectations for students in most states. They will need additional support to ensure that they are capable of teaching all students to meet the Standards.

Common Core State Standards can strengthen professional development. Now, many experts travel around the country offering workshops for teachers, but because each state has its own standards, the topics of these workshops are often generic—cooperative learning, say, or differentiated instruction. Research on professional development, however, suggests that such learning is more effective in improving instruction if it is tied to the actual content teachers teach. With common standards, national experts can focus on the same content wherever they happen to be.

At the same time, the Common Core State Standards also open up greater possibilities for online professional development. Just as students can benefit from digital resources no matter where they happen to live, so can teachers. They can take advantage of materials and resources that are aligned to the Common Core State Standards. Expert teachers can use online availability to share their expertise with other teachers in other states. The possibility for teachers to become professional development providers without leaving the classroom creates new opportunities for teachers' professional advancement. Teachers can become "teacher-preneurs."[8]

TESTS AND TEST INFORMATION

As noted in chapter 7, the tests now being developed to measure the Common Core State Standards will look considerably different from the typical state tests in use today. They will be administered at different times during the year, rather than only at the end of the year; they will incorporate extended tasks that will take place in classrooms; they will use a variety of item formats, including an extensive use of open-ended tasks that ask students to write responses, rather than solely multiple-choice items; and they will be administered on computers and will include tasks that involve the use of technology to manipulate data and respond to test questions. To perform well on these assessments, students will need considerable experience in using technology, in writing and responding to open-ended questions; and in performing extended tasks, among other skills. These assessments will therefore exert a considerable influence on instructional practice.

The tests will also provide different information for students, parents, teachers, and members of the community. They are expected to show, for example, whether students are on track toward college and career readiness, not merely whether the students have attained "proficiency." Toward that end, they might show what knowledge and skills a student can demonstrate, and which she needs to master in order to get on track toward college and career readiness. Such information is much more powerful and useful than a simple score that says little about what a student needs to do to improve.

The assessments will also be comparable across states. In that way, a parent in Ohio will know whether her child's performance is as high as that of a student in nearby Kentucky—something not possible today. Similarly, principals and teachers will be able to compare their school's performance to that of similar schools in other states and, if they are lower, can visit the schools to find out what they are doing to be more successful.

In addition to the comprehensive assessments, the assessments that will be developed for students with disabilities and for English language proficiency will also provide, for the first time, common policies for those populations. Currently, each state has its own alternate assessment, with "alternate achievement standards," for students with severe disabilities who cannot take regular assessments. Like the regular assessments and standards, these assessments and standards vary widely across states. The common assessments the state consortia are developing would end these variations and set common expectations for students with disabilities.

Likewise, the common English language proficiency assessments would eliminate variations in standards for English language learners. A student who is proficient in English in California, for example, will have to demonstrate the same language skills as a student in New Mexico.

OBSTACLES AHEAD

While all of these changes are possible, there are a number of obstacles that stand in the way of realizing them. Unless these obstacles are addressed, the Common Core State Standards will end up having a modest impact on school practice and student learning, just as previous generations of standards did.

Changing Leadership in the States

Leaders of the Common Core effort recognized that state leadership was critical to ensuring its success. Only if top officials in each state committed their support for the effort could it take off. So they required each governor and chief state school officer to sign the memorandum of agreement to participate in the process of developing the Standards. And, remarkably, forty-eight governors and forty-eight state chiefs signed. Then state boards and chiefs in forty-three states and the District of Columbia adopted the standards.

The 2010 elections brought in a new crop of state leaders, however. Because of term limits, retirements, and electoral defeats, twenty-nine new governors took office in January 2011, the largest group of new chief executives in decades. And twenty-four new state chiefs also took office after the election.

These new leaders for the most part have no history with the Common Core State Standards. Politicians prefer to create their own initiatives, rather than carry out the initiatives their predecessors launched. So the Common Core leaders have a formidable task ahead to educate these new governors and chief state school officers and make sure they implement the new standards.

At the same time, the leaders also face the challenge of building a broader base of support for the Standards. For the most part, as one leader of the effort put it, support for the Standards is a "mile wide and an inch deep," echoing a frequent criticism leveled at the U.S. school curriculum. State officials and education policy leaders have been deeply immersed in the effort, and they generally back it. But not many teachers, parents, or members of the general public are even aware of the Common Core State Standards. Some national organizations, such as the National PTA and the National Education Association, have taken steps to inform the broader public about the Standards and what they mean, and many states also intend to do so as part of their implementation efforts. But they need to do more so that the Standards maintain their wide reach and produce their intended effects.

The Funding Crunch

Perhaps the most significant obstacle is funding. States adopted the new standards at one of the bleakest budget times in recent memory. As of this writing, nearly every state is looking to cut spending and raise revenue in order to plug gaping deficits, yet many of the initiatives the Common Core State Standards call for will require some funding. For example, as noted in chapter 7, the new assessments will cost money to administer, even though the federal government paid for their development, and in some cases, the cost might be higher than states are now paying. In addition, the substantial professional development required to bring teachers up to speed on the Common Core State Standards and ensure that they can teach them effectively will require states and districts to provide significant support to teachers.

The Common Core State Standards can help mitigate some of these expenses, however. The fact that nearly all the states have adopted them and face the same challenges means that states can find creative ways to pool resources and provide additional services at reduced expense. The three New England states that formed the New England Common Assessment Program, for example, found that they could develop and administer their tests at much lower cost than they would have paid had they developed tests on their own. A study of the cost of assessments found that if states participate in consortia, they can substantially reduce their costs by reducing overhead expenses and strengthening their ability to negotiate lower rates from test vendors.[9] Similarly, combining efforts to provide professional development support to teachers can also reduce costs.

Technology can also help lower costs. Online testing can substantially reduce expenses by sharply reducing the cost associated with distributing and collecting test materials. In addition, computer scoring eliminates the expenses associated with bringing together teachers and other trained individuals to score test items. While states might want to maintain some human scoring, because of the professional development value it brings, they can enable teachers to score tests on computers, rather than bring them together in person, or hold face-to-face scoring sessions on a small scale.

At the same time, online professional development is much less expensive and potentially more effective than large workshops where teachers listen to experts in hotel ballrooms—a common format. Not only do the online tutorials eliminate the travel costs; they also give teachers opportunities to work at their own pace and on their own time. They can learn when they need to, rather than wait for the half-day on Wednesday when they will meet with their colleagues after school.

Alignment

Another challenge to the potential of the Common Core State Standards is the alignment among the Standards and the tests, curriculum materials, and professional development that are expected to support them. Teachers might teach to the standards, but if the tests do not measure what the standards expect, teachers will likely be tempted to emphasize what is tested, rather than the Standards. And the test results will not provide a true picture of student progress toward the Standards.

Likewise, curriculum materials that do not match the Standards leave teachers in a bind. They could follow the materials and not enable their students to learn what the Standards expect of them. And professional development needs to align with the Standards' expectations as well, so that teachers learn what they need to help their students succeed.

Alignment is difficult to achieve, and historically, it has not always been achieved. As noted in chapter 1, studies of alignment between state tests and standards have shown consistently that the tests generally do not measure the breadth of the standards and, in most cases, fail to address the cognitive complexity the standards expect students to demonstrate.[10] In addition, textbooks and

173

other curriculum materials often do not match the standards, despite publishers' claims. Often, publishers make only minor modifications to their existing materials to say that they have aligned to state or national standards.

There is reason for optimism this time around, however. The consortia developing assessments to measure the Common Core State Standards are working closely from the outset with the writers of the Standards, helping to ensure that the assessments do in fact measure what the Standards expect. And, again, the fact that the Standards have been adopted in nearly all states provides a powerful incentive for publishers to develop materials that genuinely reflect the Standards, rather than make superficial changes so that they can continue to sell materials nationwide.

Governance

A fourth challenge to the Common Core State Standards is the governance of the enterprise. Up to now, the effort has been led by the Council of Chief State School Officers (CCSSO) and the National Governors Association (NGA). This arrangement has enabled the effort to move forward and produce the document described in chapter 4. It has ensured that the effort has been state-run, rather than acquiring the color of federal involvement. And as Roy Romer, the former governor of Colorado and former superintendent of the Los Angeles Unified School District, once put it, it has enabled the effort succeed because it didn't have a visible leader who could be a target.

Whether this arrangement is sustainable is unclear. The CCSSO and NGA have a number of priorities beyond the Common Core, and the Standards will require some decisions that might need dedicated attention. For example, states might want an entity that will ensure that tests and curriculum materials are aligned to the Standards. In addition, the Standards will have to be revised at some point, as new research on college and career readiness points to new knowledge and skills that students should develop or suggests that some of the Standards might not be essential. Someone will have to monitor this research and oversee the revision process (and the subsequent re-adoption process).

To consider possible governance models, the Thomas B. Fordham Institute in 2010 invited eighteen policy makers and researchers to suggest how the project can move forward. They came up with three possibilities:

- "Let's become more like France." Under that scenario, a formal entity is created that oversees standards, assessments, and implementation.
- "Don't rock the boat." The states continue to oversee the effort and leave alignment to the market; when the standards need to be revised, the CCSSO and NGA will convene another group of writers.
- "One foot before the other." An interim body is created that shares information, while states lead implementation efforts. Over time, this body might become permanent and oversee the revisions of the standards.[11]

The Fordham report favored the third option. The first model appeared too bold, and the second too passive. "Model #3 creates a modest, forward-looking, yet impermanent entity that would do useful things during this sensitive period and help shape the longer haul," the report concludes.[12] The report recommends the creation of an interim coordinating council that would track and report on state implementation efforts; foster interstate collaboration and coordination; prepare for the eventual revision of the standards and inclusion of other subject areas; work toward greater understanding and buy-in by other sectors; and recommend a long-term governance arrangement.

The CCSSO and NGA strongly objected to this recommendation. In a statement, they warned that it would perhaps involve the federal government, when the effort should continue to be state-led. And they suggested that the tasks ahead were narrower than the Fordham report proposed and should be limited to monitoring adoption and overseeing future activities.

STANDARDS AND INNOVATION

The Common Core State Standards are not the only reform movement under way in the United States. There is at the same time a burgeoning interest in innovation in education and in allowing schools the freedom and flexibility to try new approaches and expand the boundaries of traditional schooling.

Charter schools are the most visible sign of this movement. There are now more than five thousand charter schools in forty states and the District of Columbia. While not all charter schools are "innovative," many have used the flexibility of charter laws to create schools that operate very differently from conventional schools.

Even as it cheered on the Common Core State Standards, the Obama administration sought to encourage such innovation both by supporting the growth of charter schools and by creating the Investing in Innovation (i3) program, a $650 million fund that provided grants on a competitive basis to school districts and nonprofit organizations that proposed to create new programs and new forms of schooling. In announcing the forty-nine winners of the grants on August 5, 2010, Arne Duncan said: "All across America, innovative entrepreneurs are finding solutions to our most pressing educational challenges. i3 will support creative thinkers who test good ideas and take proven approaches to scale so that more children can benefit."[13]

Some educators have expressed concern that the Common Core State Standards could constrain innovation by requiring schools to follow a particular path. For example, Frederick Hess, an influential and prolific commentator, has questioned the effect of the Standards on innovations like School of One, a mathematics program in three New York City schools that provides an individualized program for each student by making fine-grained determinations about his or her mathematical proficiency and tying it to learning needs. Hess suggests that the assessments currently being developed to measure progress toward the Common Core State Standards could steer schools toward a particular scope and sequence. He warns that Standards advocates who have pushed for a common curriculum could move schools even further toward standard-ization, thus thwarting innovation. And he suggests that charter school advocates and education innovators have not yet envisioned these implications. He writes:

> What's the issue? After all, since *A Nation at Risk*, choice and stan-dards-based accountability have operated as the complementary pillars of school reform. In theory, test-based accountability was a mechanism for ensuring that schools were performing, making it possible to reduce micromanagement, slash regulation, and boost school autonomy.
>
> Now, in practice, any standardized assessment system is going to be constraining to some extent (by requiring that schools teach certain skills or materials in the course of a given year), but charter schools and choice advocates have largely made their peace with that kind of accountability. What's unsettling about the Common Core push is how much more intrusive the assessments and prescriptions appear to be getting, without anyone having really thought through the consequences.[14]

In expressing these concerns, Hess echoes the late Theodore Sizer, who had cautioned that standards implemented in the 1990s could thwart school efforts to design their own programs that met their own students' needs. Sizer, who had created a network of high schools known as the Coalition of Essential Schools, argued that school communities, not school districts or states, needed to de-velop their own standards. "The issue for me . . . ," Sizer wrote, "is, rather, a matter of philosophy, of intellectual freedom. How much control should the state have over a child's mind? Is there a limit to state authority here?"[15]

Almost no one would argue against innovation, and few would argue against the need for schools to have the flexibility to meet the needs of their students. But to reject standards in favor of innova-tion and flexibility could be dangerous, for several reasons. First, not all innovations are effective. Without standards and accountability for meeting the standards, parents and members of the community would have no way of knowing what the most effective approaches are and would have no way of guarding against ones that were ineffective. Little evidence shows that a free market would reward the best approaches and shun the ineffective ones.

Second, a system that enables some schools to innovate without creating standards for all invites inequities. There is no reason to believe that all schools will be innovative. Why should some students get to benefit from these innovations—assuming they are effective—while the rest languish?

That does not mean that the nation or the states should abandon or curb innovation; quite the opposite. Rather, the states should provide a floor so that all students learn at least what they need to know and be able to do, while allowing innovations that improve the way students learn to flourish.

Since the beginning—indeed, even before; the first national statute requiring public education was the Northwest Ordinance of 1787, which predated the U.S. Constitution—the United States has acted on the belief that all students deserve at least a basic education. Such an imperative is embedded in the constitution of virtually every state. For the past two decades, states have defined the meaning of a basic education in quite specific terms by establishing standards for what all students should know and be able to do. Now, with the adoption of the Common Core State Standards, nearly all the states have gone a step farther and defined what students should learn based on evidence of what they need to know to go on to college and the workplace and what the highest-performing nations expect of their students. The Standards represent a compact between the states and their citizens— if students do what they need to do to meet the standards, they will be able to succeed once they graduate. The Standards also set high expectations for states and school districts, and suggest that they need to do whatever it takes to support students and their schools.

The importance of the Standards is that, for the first time, expectations are the same for all students, regardless of their backgrounds or where they live. The promise of such a step is too great to let it slip through our fingers.

APPENDIX A

RESOURCES ON THE COMMON
CORE STATE STANDARDS

THE STANDARDS

To read the standards themselves, as well as appendixes, background information, and information on state adoption, see the Common Core State Standards Web site, www.corestandards.org.

NEWS ABOUT STANDARDS

The best source of news on the Standards is *Education Week*'s Curriculum Matters blog, where Catherine Gewertz is on top of every development. See: http://blogs.edweek.org/edweek/curriculum/.

SUPPORTING ORGANIZATIONS

Organizations supporting the Common Core State Standards have posted a wealth of information on the Standards and their adoption and implementation. See the Alliance for Excellent Education's Common Standards portal, http://all4ed.org/common-standards; the James B. Hunt Jr. Institute for Educational

Leadership and Policy, http://www.hunt-institute.org/education-initiatives/shaping-rigorous-world-class-standards/; Achieve, http://www.achieve.org/standards-0; and the Thomas B. Fordham Institute, which includes an archive of the Institute's reports rating state standards since 1998, http://www.edexcellence.net/publications-issues/standards-testing-accountability.html.

ASSESSMENT CONSORTIA

The two consortia of states developing assessments to measure the Common Core State Standards have a wealth of information on their web sites about their plans and activities. See the Partnership for Assessment of Readiness for College and Careers site: www.parcconline.org; and the Smarter Balanced Assessment Consortium site: http://www.k12.wa.us/SMARTER/.

RESEARCH ON STANDARDS

The National Research Council held two workshops, funded by the James B. Hunt Jr. Institute for Educational Policy and Leadership, to examine research on standards and assessments. A summary of the standards workshops is available at: http://books.nap.edu/catalog.php?record_id=12462; a summary of the assessment workshop is available at: http://books.nap.edu/catalog.php?record_id=13013.

APPENDIX B

COMMON CORE STATE STANDARDS K–12 WORK TEAMS AND FEEDBACK GROUPS

MATHEMATICS WORK TEAM

Beth Aune
Director of Academic Standards
and P-16 Initiatives
Minnesota Department of
Education

Deborah Loewenberg Ball
Dean, School of Education
University of Michigan

Nancy Beben
Director, Curriculum Standards
Louisiana Department of
Education

Sybilla Beckmann
Professor of Mathematics
University of Georgia

Stacey Caruso-Sharpe
Mathematics Teacher, Lynch
Literacy Academy Board of
Directors, New York State United
Teachers Vice President, American
Federation of Teachers

Diana Ceja
Teacher on Assignment
Garey High School
Pomona, California

Marta Civil
Professor
The University of Arizona

Douglas H. Clements
SUNY Distinguished Professor
University at Buffalo,
The State University of New York
Department of Learning and
Instruction, Graduate School of
Education

Thomas Coy
Public School Program Advisor
Arkansas Department of
Education

Phil Daro
America's Choice and Strategic
Education Research Partnerships

Ellen Delaney
Associate Principal
Spring Lake Park High School
Spring Lake Park, Minnesota

Susan Eddins
Faculty Emerita, Illinois
Mathematics and Science Academy
Educational Consultant

Wade Ellis
Mathematics Instructor, Retired
West Valley College

Francis (Skip) Fennell
Professor, Education Department
McDaniel College
Past-President, NCTM

Bradford R. Findell
Mathematics Initiatives
Administrator
Ohio Department of Education

Sol Garfunkel
Executive Director
COMAP, the Consortium for
Mathematics and Its Applications

Dewey Gottlieb
Education Specialist for
Mathematics
Hawaii Department of Education

Lawrence Gray
Professor of Mathematics
University of Minnesota

Kenneth I. Gross
Professor of Mathematics and
Education
University of Vermont

Denny Gulick
Professor of Mathematics
University of Maryland

Roger Howe
Wm. Kenan Jr. Professor of
Mathematics
Yale University

Deborah Hughes Hallett
Professor of Mathematics
University of Arizona
Adjunct Professor of Public Policy
Harvard Kennedy School

Linda Kaniecki
Mathematics Specialist
Maryland State Department of
Education

Mary Knuck
Deputy Associate Superintendent
Standards-Based Best Practices
Arizona Department of Education

Barbara J. Libby
STEM Director
Office for Mathematics, Science
and Technology/Engineering
Massachusetts Department of
Elementary and Secondary
Education

James Madden
Professor of Mathematics
Louisiana State University

Bernard L. Madison
Professor of Mathematics
University of Arkansas

William McCallum
Lead, Mathematics Head,
Department of Mathematics,
The University of Arizona
Senior Consultant to Achieve

Ken Mullen
Senior Mathematics Program
Development Associate
ACT

Chuck Pack
National Board Certified Teacher
(NBCT)
Mathematics Department Chair
Mathematics Curriculum
Coordinator
Tahlequah Public Schools District
Board of Directors, Oklahoma
Education Association

Becky Pittard
National Board Certified Teacher
(NBCT)
Pine Trail Elementary School
Volusia County Schools, Florida

Barbara J. Reys
Lois Knowles Distinguished
Professor of Mathematics Education
University of Missouri – Columbia

Katherine Richard
Associate Director, Mathematics
Programs
Lesley University

Deb Romanek
Director, Mathematics Education
Nebraska Department of
Education

Bernadette Sandruck
Professor & Division Chair
Mathematics
Howard Community College
Columbia, Maryland

Richard Scheaffer
Professor Emeritus
University of Florida

Andrew Schwartz
Assessment Manager, Research &
Development
The College Board

Rick Scott
P-20 Policy and Programs
New Mexico Department of Higher
Education

Carolyn Sessions
Standards and Curriculum
Projects Coordinator
Louisiana Department of
Education

Laura McGiffert Slover
Vice President, Content and Policy
Research
Achieve

Douglas Sovde
Senior Associate, Mathematics
Achieve

Sharyn Sweeney
Mathematics Standards and
Curriculum Coordinator
Massachusetts Department of
Elementary and Secondary
Education

Mary Jane Tappen
Deputy Chancellor for
Curriculum, Instruction and
Student Services
Florida Department of Education

Mark Thames
Assistant Research Scientist
School of Education
University Michigan

Patrick Thompson
Professor of Mathematics
Education
School of Mathematical and
Statistical Sciences
Arizona State University

Donna Watts
Coordinator for Mathematics and
STEM Initiatives
Maryland State Department of
Education

Kerri White
Executive Director of High School
Reform
Oklahoma State Department of
Education

Vern Williams
Mathematics Teacher
H. W. Longfellow Middle School
Fairfax County, Virginia

Hung-Hsi Wu
Professor of Mathematics, Emeritus
Department of Mathematics
University of California- Berkeley

Susan Wygant
Mathematics Specialist
Minnesota Department of
Education

Jason Zimba
Professor of Mathematics and
Physics,
Bennington College
Student Achievement Partners

MATHEMATICS FEEDBACK GROUP

Richard Askey
Professor Emeritus of Mathematics
University of Wisconsin-Madison

Hyman Bass
Samuel Eilenberg Distinguished
Univerity
Professor of Mathematics &
Mathematics Education
University of Michigan

Elaine Carman
Middle School Math Instructional
Specialist
Department of Science, Technology,
Engineering and Mathematics
Office of Curriculum, Standards
and Academic Engagement
New York City Department of
Education

Andrew Chen
President
EduTron Corporation

Miguel Cordero
Secondary Math Instructional
Specialist
Department of Science, Technology,
Engineering and Mathematics
Office of Curriculum, Standards
and Academic Engagement
New York City Department of
Education

Linda Curtis-Bey
Director, Department of Science,
Technology,
Engineering and Mathematics
Office of Curriculum, Standards
and Academic Engagement
New York City Department of
Education

John A. Dossey
Distinguished University Professor
ofMathematics Emeritus
Illinois State University

Scott Eddins
Tennessee Mathematics
Coordinator President,
Association of State Supervisors of
Mathematics (ASSM)

Lisa Emond
Elementary Math Instructional
Specialist
Department of Science, Technology,
Engineering and Mathematics
Office of Curriculum, Standards
and Academic Engagement
New York City Department of
Education

Karen Fuson
Professor Emerita
Northwestern University

Sandra Jenoure
Early Childhood Math
Instructional Specialist
Department of Science, Technology,
Engineering and Mathematics
Office of Curriculum, Standards
and Academic Engagement
New York City Department of
Education

Tammy Jones
Content Editor
Tennessee Standards Committee

Suzanne Lane
Professor, Research Methodology
Program
School of Education
University of Pittsburgh

Fabio Milner
Director, Mathematics for STEM
Education
School of Mathematical and
Statistical Sciences
Arizona State University

Jodie Olivo
5th Grade Teacher
Nathanael Greene Elementary
School
Pawtucket School Department
North Providence, Rhode Island

Roxy Peck
Associate Dean and Professor of
Statistics
College of Science and Mathematics
California Polytechnic State
University, San Luis Obispo

John Santangelo
New England Laborers'/ Cranston
Public Schools Construction
Career Academy, American
Federation of Teachers,
Rhode Island Federation of
Teachers and Health
Professionals, Cranston Teachers'
Alliance

Wilfried Schmid
Professor, Mathematics
Harvard University

Ronald Schwarz
High School Math Instructional
Specialist
Department of Science, Technology,
Engineering and Mathematics
Office of Curriculum, Standards
and Academic Engagement
New York City Department of
Education

Matthew Ting
Mathematics Instructional Coach
Los Angeles Unified School
District

Uri Treisman
Professor of Mathematics and of
Public Affairs
Executive Director
Charles A. Dana Center
The University of Texas at Austin

W. Stephen Wilson
Professor of Mathematics
Department of Mathematics
Johns Hopkins University

ENGLISH LANGUAGE ARTS WORK TEAM

Marilyn Jager Adams
Research Professor
Department of Cognitive and
Linguistic Sciences
Brown University

Marcia Ashhurst-Whiting
Language Arts Literacy Coordinator
Division of Educational Standards
and Programs
New Jersey Department of Education

Sorel Berman
English Teacher, Retired
Brookline High School
Brookline, MA

Katherine Bishop
National Board Certified Teacher
(NBCT)
Exceptional Needs Educator
Putnam City Public Schools
National Education Association
Oklahoma City, Oklahoma

Dana Breitweiser
English Language Arts Curriculum
Specialist
Arkansas Department of Education

David Buchanan
Project Manager – ESE
Performance
Standards Project
Office of Humanities
Center for Curriculum and Instruction
Massachusetts Department of
Elementary and Secondary
Education

Paul Carney
Coordinator of Ready or Not
Writing and Step
Write Up programs for the Center
for College Readiness
English Instructor
Minnesota State Community and
Technical College

David Coleman
President
Student Achievement Partners

Patricia D'Alfonso
English/Language Arts Specialist/
Coach
West Warwick Public Schools
West Warwick, RI

Janet Davis
Point Professional Development
Advisor
Los Angeles Unified School District

Matthew Davis
Director, Reading Program
Core Knowledge Foundation

Steve Delvecchio
Librarian
Seattle, Washington

JoAnne T. Eresh
Senior Associate for English
Language Arts
Achieve

Jan Freeland
Middle and Secondary English
Language Arts Supervisor
Middle and Secondary Standards
Louisiana Department of Education

Sally Hampton
Senior Fellow
America's Choice and Strategic
Education Research Partnerships

Juley Harper
ELA Education Associate,
Curriculum and Instruction
Delaware Department of Education

Joel Harris
Director, English Language Arts
Curriculum and Standards,
Research and Development,
The College Board

Bobbi Ciriza Houtchens
U.S. Department of Education
Teaching
Ambassador Fellow (2009)
Teacher & English Language
Facilitator
Arroyo Valley High School
San Bernardino, CA

Michael Kamil
Professor, Language Learning and
Policy
Stanford University School of
Education

Valerie Kinloch
Associate Professor, Literacy Studies
School of Teaching and Learning
The Ohio State University

Karen Klinzing
Assistant Commissioner
Minnesota Department of
Education

Susan Lafond
National Board Certified Teacher
(NBCT) in English as a New
Language (EAYA ENL)
Assistant in Educational Services
New York State United Teachers

Carol D. Lee
Professor of Learning Sciences &
African American Studies
Northwestern University President
American Educational Research
Association

David Liben
Liben Education Consulting L. L. C.

Meredith Liben
Liben Education Consulting L.L.C.

Cheryl Liebling
Director, Office of Literacy
Massachusetts Department of
Elementary and Secondary
Education

James Marshall
Associate Dean of Academic
Programs
Professor of Language and Literacy
Education
University of Georgia

Margaret McKeown
Senior Scientist Learning Research
and Development Center
Clinical Professor, Instruction and
Learning
School of Education
University of Pittsburgh

Nina Metzner
Senior Test Development Associate
in Language Arts
ACT

Louisa Moats
Moats Associates Consulting, Inc

Laura Mongello
Vice President, Product Development
The Quarasan Group, Inc

Sandra M. Murphy
Professor Emerita
University of California, Davis

Jim Patterson
Senior Program Development
Associate in Language Arts
ACT, Inc.

Anthony Petrosky
Professor of Education/ Professor
of English & Associate Dean for
Academic Program
School of Education
University of Pittsburgh

Julia Phelps
Director of Curriculum &
Instruction
Massachusetts Department of
Elementary & Secondary Education

Susan Pimentel
Lead, English Language Arts
Senior Consultant to Achieve

Donlynn Rice
Administrator, Curriculum,
Instruction, and Innovation
Nebraska Department of
Education

Ricardo Rincón
Sunrise Elementary Teacher
University of Phoenix Faculty
and Mentor
National ELL Training Cadre

Tracy Robertson
English Coordinator
Virginia Department of Education

Kari D. Ross
Reading Specialist
Division of School Improvement
Minnesota Department of Education

Petra Schatz
Educational Specialist
Language Arts, Instructional
Sevices Branch
Office of Curriculum, Instruction
& Student Support
Hawaii Department of Education

Diana Senechal
Author
ELA and ESL certified
New York State

Timothy Shanahan
Professor of Urban Education
University of Illinois at Chicago

Miriam Soto-Pressley
Elementary Teacher
American Federation of Teachers
ELL Cadre Committee
Hammond, Indiana

Laura McGiffert Slover
Vice President, Content and Policy
Research
Achieve

Charon Tierney
Language Arts Specialist
Minnesota Department of Education

Vince Verges
Executive Director
Test Development Center
Florida Department of Education

Elaine Weber
Consultant
Macomb ISD Michigan

Susan Wheltle
Director, Office for Humanities,
History and Social Science
Center for Curriculum and
Instruction
Massachusetts Department of
Elementary and Secondary
Education

Karen Wixson
Professor of Education
University of Michigan

ENGLISH LANGUAGE ARTS FEEDBACK GROUP

Mark Bauerlein
Department of English,
Emory University

Gina Biancarosa
Assistant Professor of Special
Education
University of Oregon, College of
Education

Sheila Byrd Carmichael
Education Policy Consultant

Erika Cassel
National Board Certified Teacher
(NBCT)
Humanities Teacher
Central Kitsap Junior High

Barbara R. Foorman
Francis Eppes Professor of
Education Director
Florida Center for Reading Research
Florida State University

Juley Harper
ELA Education Associate,
Curriculum and Instruction
Delaware Department of
Education

George Kamberelis
Wyoming Excellence Chair of
Literacy Education
College of Education
University of Wyoming

Deborah D. Perry
Director of K–12 ELA
Arlington, Massachusetts Public
Schools

Cheryl M. Scott
Professor
Department of Communication
Disorders and Sciences
Rush University Medical Center

Doranna Tindle
Instructional Performance Coach
Friendship Public Charter School
Clinton, MD

Marc Tucker
President
National Center on Education and
the Economy

Arlette Ingram
Willis Professor
University of Illinois

APPENDIX C

COMMON CORE STATE STANDARDS VALIDATION COMMITTEE

Bryan Albrecht, President, Gateway Technical College, Kenosha, Wisconsin

Arthur Applebee, Distinguished Professor, Center on English Learning & Achievement, School of Education, University at Albany, SUNY

Sarah Baird, 2009 Arizona Teacher of the Year, K-5 Math Coach, Kyrene School District

Jere Confrey, Joseph D. Moore Distinguished University Professor, William and Ida Friday Institute for Educational Innovation, College of Education, North Carolina State University

David T. Conley, Professor, College of Education, University of Oregon CEO, Educational Policy Improvement Center **(Co-Chair)**

Linda Darling-Hammond, Charles E. Ducommun Professor of Education, Stanford University

Alfinio Flores, Hollowell Professor of Mathematics Education, University of Delaware

Brian Gong, Executive Director, Center for Assessment **(Co-Chair)**

Kenji Hakuta, Lee L. Jacks Professor of Education, Stanford University

Kristin Buckstad Hamilton, Teacher, Battlefield Senior High School, NEA

Feng-Jui Hsieh, Associate Professor of the Mathematics Department, National Taiwan Normal University

Mary Ann Jordan, Teacher, New York City Dept of Education, AFT

Jeremy Kilpatrick, Regents Professor of Mathematics Education, University of Georgia

Jill Martin, Principal, Pine Creek High School

Barry McGaw, Professor and Director of Melbourne Education Research Institute, University of Melbourne; Director for Education, OECD

James Milgram, Professor Emeritus, Stanford University

P. David Pearson, Professor and Dean, Graduate School of Education, University of California, Berkeley

Steve Pophal, Principal, DC Everest Junior High

Stanley Rabinowitz, Senior Program Director, Assessment and Standards Development Services, WestEd

Lauren Resnick, Distinguished University Professor, Psychology and Cognitive Science, Learning Sciences and Education Policy, University of Pittsburgh

Andreas Schleicher, Head, Indicators and Analysis Division of the OECD Directorate for Education

William Schmidt, University Distinguished Professor, Michigan State University

Catherine Snow, Henry Lee Shattuck Professor of Education, Harvard Graduate School of Education

Christopher Steinhauser, Superintendent of Schools, Long Beach Unified School District

Sandra Stotsky, Professor of Education Reform, 21st Century Chair in Teacher Quality, University of Arkansas

Dorothy Strickland, Samuel DeWitt Proctor Professor of Ed., Emerita, Distinguished Research Fellow, National Institute for Early Education Research, Rutgers, The State University of NJ

Martha Thurlow, Director, National Center on Educational Outcomes, University of Minnesota

Norman Webb, Senior Research Scientist, Emeritus, Wisconsin Center for Education Research, University of Wisconsin

Dylan William, Deputy Director, Institute of Education, University of London

NOTES

Introduction

1. Quoted in Lynn Olson, "Off and Running," in *From Risk to Renewal: Charting a Course for Reform*, eds. Editors of *Education Week* (Washington, DC: Editorial Projects in Education, 1993), 169.

Chapter 1

1. Jack Markell, Remarks at Release of Common Core State Standards, June 2, 2010, http://www.corestandards.org/articles/8-national-governors-association-and-state-education-chiefs-launch-common-state-academic-standards.

2. Eric Smith, Remarks at Release of Common Core State Standards, June 2, 2010, http://www.corestandards.org/articles/8-national-governors-association-and-state-education-chiefs-launch-common-state-academic-standards.

3. William H. Schmidt, Curtis C. McKnight, Richard T. Houang, Hsing Chi Wang, David E. Wiley, Leland S. Cogan, and Richard G. Wolfe, *Why Schools Matter: A Cross-National Comparison of Curriculum and Learning* (San Francisco: Jossey-Bass, 2001).

4. Arne Duncan, Remarks at 2009 Governors Education Symposium, June 14, 2009, http://www2.ed.gov/news/speeches/2009/06/06142009.html.

5. Lauren B. Resnick, "From Aptitude to Effort: A New Foundation for Our Schools," *Daedalus* 124, no. 4 (Fall 1995): 55–62.

6. Marshall S. Smith and Jennifer O'Day, "Systemic School Reform," in *The Politics of Curriculum and Testing: The 1990 Yearbook of the Politics of Education Association*, eds. S. H. Fuhrman and B. Malen (Bristol, PA: Falmer Press, 1991), 233–268.

7. Bobby D. Rampey, Gloria S. Dion, and Patricia L. Donohue, *NAEP 2008 Trends in Academic Progress* (NCES 2009–479) (Washington, DC: National Center for Education Statistics, Institute of Education Sciences, U.S. Department of Education, April 2009).

8. Grover Whitehurst, *Don't Forget Curriculum*, Brown Center Letters on Education, October 2009, http://www.brookings.edu/~/media/Files/rc/papers/2009/1014_curriculum_whitehurst/1014_curriculum_whitehurst.pdf.

9. Ibid., 7.

10. See, for example, Daniel Koretz, Karen Mitchell, Sheila Barron, and S. Keith, *Perceived Effects of the Maryland State Assessment Program* (Technical Report No. 406) (Los Angeles: University of California, Los Angeles, National Center for Research on Evaluation, Standards, and Student Testing, 1996); Lorraine McDonnell and C. Choiser, *Testing and teaching: Local Implementation of New State Assessments* (Technical Report No. 442) (Los Angeles: University of California, Los Angeles, National Center for Research on Evaluation, Standards, and Student Testing, 1997); Cynthia E. Coburn, "Collective sensemaking about reading: How teachers mediate reading policy in their professional communities," *Educational Evaluation and Policy Analysis* 23, no. 2 (2001): 145–170.

11. James P. Spillane, *Standards Deviation: How Schools Misunderstand Education Policy* (Cambridge, MA: Harvard University Press, 2004).

12. Brian Stecher and Hilda Borko, *Combining Surveys and Case Studies to Examine Standards-Based Educational Reform* (CSE Technical Report 565) (Los Angeles: University of California, National Center for Research on Evaluation, Standards, and Student Testing, 2002).

13. Robert Rothman, "Benchmarking and Alignment of State Standards and Assessments," in *Redesigning Accountability Systems for Education*, eds. Susan H. Fuhrman and Richard F. Elmore (New York: Teachers College Press, 2004), 96–114; Robert Rothman, Jean Slattery, Jennifer Vranek, and Lauren B. Resnick, *Benchmarking and Alignment of Standards and Testing* (Los Angeles: National Center for Research on Evaluation, Standards, and Student Testing, 2002).

14. Tom Toch, *Margins of Error* (Washington, DC: Education Sector, 2006).

15. Richard F. Elmore and Robert Rothman, eds., *Testing, Teaching and Learning: A Guide for States and School Districts* (Washington, DC: National Academy Press, 1999), 20.

16. Whitehurst, *What About Curriculum?*

17. Diana Senechal, "The Spark of Specifics: How a Strong Curriculum Enlivens Classroom and School Culture," *American Educator* 34, no. 4 (Winter 2010–11): 24–29, 54.

18. Linda Darling-Hammond, *The Flat World and Education* (New York: Teachers College Press, 2010).

19. Diane Ravitch, *The Language Police* (New York: Alfred A. Knopf, 2003), 103.

20. David C. Cohen and Heather Hill, *Learning Policy* (New Haven, CT: Yale University Press), 2001.

21. Laurie Lewis, Basmat Parsad, Nancy Carey, Nicole Bartfai, Elizabeth Farris, and Becky Smerdon, *Teacher Quality: A Report on the Preparation and Qualifications of Public School Teachers* (NCES 1999-080) (Washington, DC: National Center for Education Statistics, 1999).

22. Jane L. David and Patrick M. Shields, *When Theory Hits Reality: Standards-Based Reform in Urban Districts* (Philadelphia: Pew Charitable Trusts, 2001).

Chapter 2

1. National Council of Teachers of Mathematics, *Curriculum and Evaluation Standards for School Mathematics* (Reston, VA: National Council of Teachers of Mathematics, 1989), 1.

2. National Council of Teachers of Mathematics, *Curriculum and Evaluation Standards*.

3. Diane Ravitch, *National Standards in American Education: A Citizen's Guide* (Washington, DC: Brookings Institution, 1995).

4. National Council on Education Standards and Testing, *Raising Standards for American Education* (Washington, DC: U.S. Department of Education, 1992), 2–3.

5. Ravitch, *National Standards*, 29.

6. Quoted in Robert C. Johnston and Karen Diegmuller, "Senate Approves Resolution Denouncing History Standards," *Education Week*, January 25, 1995, http://www.edweek.org/ew/articles/1995/01/25/18stand.h14.html?qs=history+standards.

7. Quoted in Karen Diegmuller, "English Group Loses Funding for Standards," *Education Week*, March 30, 1994, http://www.edweek.org/ew/articles/1994/03/30/27eng.h13.html?qs=English+standards.

8. Patricia A. Lauer, David Snow, Mya Martin-Glenn, Rebecca J. Van Buhler, Kirsten Stoutemyre, and Ravay Snow-Renner, *The Influence of Standards on K–12 Teaching and Student Learning: A Research Synthesis* (Aurora, CO: McREL, August 2005).

9. Lynn Olson, "An 'A' or a 'D': State Rankings Differ Widely," *Education Week*, April 15, 1998, http://www.edweek.org/ew/articles/1998/04/15/31stand.h17.html?qs=Council+Basic+Education+standards.

10. American Federation of Teachers, *Making Standards Matter* (Washington, DC: Author, 2000).

11. Sheila Byrd Carmichael, Gabrielle Martino, Kathleen Porter-Magee, and W. Stephen Wilson, *The State of State Standards—and the Common Core—in 2010* (Washington, DC: Thomas B. Fordham Institute, July 2010).

12. Quoted in Diane Ravitch, "50 States, 50 Standards: The Continuing Need for National Voluntary Standards in Education," Washington, DC: Brookings Institution, Summer 1996, http://www.brookings.edu/articles/1996/summer_education_ravitch.aspx.

13. Quoted in David J. Hoff, "Clinton Gives Top Billing to Education Plan," *Education Week*, February 12, 1997, http://www.edweek.org/ew/articles/1997/02/12/20clint.h16.html?qs=Clinton.

14. Michael J. Feuer, Paul J. Holland, Bert F. Green, Meryl W. Bertenthal, and F. Cadell Hemphill, eds., *Uncommon Measures: Equivalence and Linkage among Educational Tests* (Washington, DC: National Academy Press, 1999).

15. Jay P. Heubert and Robert F. Hauser, eds., *High Stakes: Testing for Tracking, Promotion, and Graduation* (Washington, DC: National Academy Press, 1999).

16. John Cronin, Michael Dahlin, Deborah Atkins, and G. Gage Kingsbury, *The Proficiency Illusion* (Washington, DC: Thomas B. Fordham Institute, October 2007).

17. Kevin Carey, *Hot Air: How States Inflate their Educational Progress under NCLB* (Washington, DC: Education Sector, May 2006).

18. Goodwin Liu, "Interstate Inequality in Educational Opportunity" (paper presented at a conference sponsored by the Chief Justice Earl Warren Institute on Race, Ethnicity, and Diversity, "Key Reforms under the No Child Left Behind Act: The Civil Rights Perspective," November 16–17, 2006), http://www.law.berkeley.edu/centers/ewi-old/research/k12equity/Liu.html.

19. National Research Council, *Common Standards for K–12 Education?: Considering the Evidence. Summary of a Workshop Series* (Washington, DC: National Academies Press, 2008), 15.

20. Tom Toch, *Margins of Error: The Education Testing Industry in the No Child Left Behind Era* (Washington, DC: Education Sector, 2006).

Chapter 3

1. ACT, *Crisis at the Core: Preparing All Students for College and Work* (Iowa City, IA: ACT, 2004).

2. Thomas L. Friedman, *The World Is Flat: A Brief History of the Twenty-First Century* (New York: Farrar, Straus, and Giroux, 2005).

3. Patrick Gonzales, Christopher Calsyn, Leslie Jocelyn, Kitty Mak, David Kastberg, Sousan Arafeh, Trevor Williams, and Winnie Tsen, *Pursuing Excellence: Comparisons of Eighth Grade Mathematics and Science Achievement from a U.S. Perspective* (Washington, DC: U.S. Department of Education, National Center for Education Statistics, December 2000).

4. Mariann Lemke, Anindita Sen, Erin Pahlke, Lisette Partelow, David Miller, Trevor Williams, David Kastberg, and Leslie Jocelyn, *Outcomes of Learning in Mathematics Literacy and Problem Solving: PISA 2003 Results from the U.S. Perspective* (Washington, DC: U.S. Department of Education, National Center for Education Statistics, December 2004).

5. Personal communication, April 12, 2011.

6. Ibid.

7. Diane Massell, "The current status and role of standards-based reform in the United States" (paper prepared for the National Research Council Workshop

on Assessing the Role of K–12 Academic Standards in States, National Research Council, Washington, DC, 2008), http://www7.nationalacademies.org/cfe/Massell%20State%20Standards%20Paper.pdf; Andrew Porter, Michael Polikoff, and John Smithson, "Is there a de facto national curriculum? Evidence from state standards" (paper prepared for the National Research Council Workshop on Assessing the Role of K–12 Academic Standards), http://www7.nationalacademies.org/cfe/Porter_Smithson%20State%20Standards%20Paper_Tables.pdf; and Margaret Goertz, "Identifying the costs of standards-based K–12 education" (presentation to the National Research Council Workshop on Assessing the Role of K–12 Academic Standards in States), http://www7.nationalacademies.org/cfe/Goertz%20State%20Standards%20Presentation.pdf.

8. National Research Council, *Common Standards for K–12 Education? Considering the Evidence: Summary of a Workshop Series* (Washington, DC: National Academies Press, 2008), 73.

9. Hunt Institute, "World-Class Standards; Setting a New Cornerstone for American Education," *Hunt Institute's Blueprint for Education Leadership*, No. 2, October 2008, http://www.hunt-institute.org/elements/media/files/Blueprint_Number_2.pdf.

10. Ibid.

11. Cindy Brown and Elena Rocha, *The Case for National Standards, Accountability, and Fiscal Equity* (Washington, DC: Center for American Progress, November 2005).

12. Chester E. Finn Jr., Liam Julian, and Michael J. Petrilli, *To Dream the Impossible Dream: Four Approaches to National Standards and Tests for America's Schools* (Washington, DC: Thomas B. Fordham Foundation, August 2006).

13. Rudy Crew, Paul Vallas, and Michael Casserly, "The Case for National Standards in American Education," *Education Week* 26, no. 26 (March 5, 2007): 28, 40, http://www.edweek.org/ew/articles/2007/03/05/26crew.h26.html?qs=national+standards.

14. Margaret Spellings, "A National Test We Don't Need," *Washington Post*, June 9, 2007, A18.

15. Achieve, *Ready or Not: Creating a High School Diploma that Counts* (Washington, DC: Achieve, 2004), http://www.achieve.org/files/ADPreport_7.pdf.

16. Achieve, *Out of Many, One: Toward Rigorous Common Core Standards from the Ground Up* (Washington, DC: Achieve, July 2008), http://www.achieve.org/files/CommonCore.pdf.

17. National Governors Association, Council of Chief State School Officers, and Achieve, *Benchmarking for Success: Ensuring U.S. Students Receive a World-Class Education* (Washington, DC: National Governors Association, 2008), 6.

18. Personal communication, April 14, 2011.

19. Jay P. Greene, "The National Standards Sausage-Making," jaypgreene.com, June 9, 2009, http://jaypgreene.com/2009/06/09/the-national-standards-sausage-making/.

20. David Coleman and Jason Zimba, *Math and Science Standards that are Fewer, Clearer, and Higher to Raise Achievement at All Levels* (New York and Princeton, NJ: Carnegie Corporation of New York–Institute for Advanced Study Commission on Mathematics and Science Education, 2007).

21. Robert Pondiscio, "Voluntary National Standards Dead on Arrival," coreknowledge.org, July 22, 2009, http://blog.coreknowledge.org/2009/07/.

22. Sean Cavanaugh and Catherine Gewirtz, "Draft Content Standards Elicit Mixed Reviews," *Education Week* 28, no. 37 (July 23, 2009), http://www.edweek.org/ew/articles/2009/07/23/37standards.h28.html?tkn=NTOFlfFcwcuXOEXxZLxiBzb1yrUmfDD3NzrH.

23. Sheila Byrd Carmichael, W. Stephen Wilson, Chester E. Finn Jr., Amber E. Winkler, and Stafford Palmieri, *Stars by Which to Navigate? Scanning National and International Standards in 2009* (Washington, DC: Thomas B. Fordham Institute, October 2009), http://www.edexcellencemedia.net/publications/2009/200910_starsbywhichtonavigate/Stars%20by%20Which%20to%20Navigate%20-%20October%202009.pdf.

24. Nick Anderson, "Governors, State School Superintendents to Propose Common Academic Standards," *Washington Post*, March 10, 2010, 1.

25. New York Times, "National School Standards, at Last," *New York Times*, March 13, 2010.

26. Catherine Gewirtz, "Potential for Both Value and Harm Seen in K–3 Common Standards," *Education Week* 29, no. 28 (April 7, 2010): 1, 20, http://www.edweek.org/ew/articles/2010/04/07/28common.h29.html?qs=common+standards.

27. Alliance for Childhood, Joint Statement of Early Childhood Health and Education Professionals on the Common Core Standards Initiative (College Park, MD: Alliance for Childhood, March 16, 2010), http://www.allianceforchildhood.org/sites/allianceforchildhood.org/files/file/Joint%20Statement%20on%20Core%20Standards_%28418%20%29.pdf.

28. Sheila Byrd Carmichael, Gabrielle Martino, Kathleen Porter-Magee, and W. Stephen Wilson, *The State if State Standards—and the Common Core—in 2010* (Washington, DC: Thomas B. Fordham Institute, July 2010), http://edexcellencemedia.net/publications/2010/201007_state_education_standards_common_standards/SOSSandCC2010_FullReportFINAL.pdf.

29. National Governors Association and Council of Chief State School Officers, *Reaching Higher: The Common Core State Standards Validation Committee* (Washington, DC: National Governors Association and Council of Chief State School Officers, June 2010), http://www.corestandards.org/assets/CommonCoreReport_6.10.pdf, 3.

Chapter 4

1. Andrew C. Porter, Jennifer McMaken, Jun Hwang, and Rui Yang, "Common Core Standards: The New US Intended Curriculum" (paper prepared for a symposium sponsored by the Brookings Institution, "Race to the Top Assessments: Common Core Standards and their Impact on Student Testing," Washington, DC, October 28, 2010).

2. Tom Loveless, *The 2010 Brown Center Report on American Education: How Well are American Students Learning?* vol. II, no. 5 (Washington, DC: Brookings Institution, February 2011), http://www.brookings.edu/~/media/Files/rc/reports/2011/0207 _education_loveless/0207_education_loveless.pdf.

3. ACT, Inc., *Reading Between the Lines: What the ACT Reveals about College Readiness in Reading* (Iowa City, IA: ACT, 2006).

4. James W. Pellegrino, Naomi Chudowsky, and Robert Glaser, eds., *Knowing What Students Know* (Washington, DC: National Academy Press, 2001).

5. Council of Chief State School Officers and NGA Center for Best Practices, *Common Core State Standards for English Language Arts & Literacy in History/Social Studies, Science, and Technical Subjects*, Appendix A (Washington, DC: author, 2010), 26.

6. Carnegie Council on Advancing Adolescent Literacy, *Time to Act: An Agenda for Advancing Adolescent Literacy for College and Career Success* (New York: Carnegie Corporation of New York, 2010), 13.

7. ACT, *Reading Between the Lines.*

8. Council of Chief State School Officers and NGA Center for Best Practices, *Common Core State Standards for English Language Arts & Literacy in History/Social Studies, Science, and Technical Subjects*, Appendix A.

9. Jeanne Chall, S. Conard, and S. Harris, *An Analysis of Textbooks in Relationship to Declining SAT Scores* (Princeton, NJ: College Entrance Examination Board, 1977); D.P. Hayes, L.T. Wolfer, and M.F. Wolfe, "Sourcebook Simplification and its Relation to the Decline in SAT-Verbal Scores," *American Educational Research Journal* 33 (1996): 489–508; Gary Williamson, *Aligning the Journey with a Destination: A Model for K–16 Reading Standards* (Durham, NC: Metametrics, 2006).

10. Council of Chief State School Officers and NGA Center for Best Practices, *Common Core State Standards for English Language Arts & Literacy in History/Social Studies, Science, and Technical Subjects*, Appendix B, http://www.corestandards.org/ assets/Appendix_B.pdf, 89.

11. William H. Schmidt, Curtis C. McKnight, Richard T. Houang, Hsing Chi Wang, David E. Wiley, Leland S. Cogan, and Richard G. Wolfe, *Why Schools Matter: A Cross-National Comparison of Curriculum and Learning* (San Francisco: Jossey-Bass, 2001).

12. Council of Chief State School Officers and NGA Center for Best Practices, *Common Core State Standards for English Language Arts & Literacy in History/Social Studies, Science, and Technical Subjects*, 6.

13. Ibid., http://www.corestandards.org/the-standards/mathematics/grade-2/number-and-operations-in-base-ten/.

14. Ibid., http://www.corestandards.org/the-standards/mathematics/grade-6/expressions-and-equations/.

15. Ibid., http://www.corestandards.org/the-standards/mathematics/grade-7/expressions-and-equations/.

16. Ibid., http://www.corestandards.org/the-standards/mathematics/high-school-modeling/introduction/.

17. Ibid., Appendix A, 5.

Chapter 5

1. Council of Chief State School Officers and Learning Point Associates, *Preliminary Review: CCSSO Strategic Initiatives Identified in Phase 1 Race to the Top Applications* (Naperville, IL: Learning Point Associates, March 2010), http://www.learningpt.org/pdfs/RttT_Preliminary_Review.pdf.

2. Center on Education Policy, *States' Progress and Challenges in Implementing Common Core State Standards* (Washington, DC: Center on Education Policy, January 2011).

3. Barack Obama, *Remarks by the President in State of Union Address*, January 25, 2011, http://www.whitehouse.gov/the-press-office/2011/01/25/remarks-president-state-union-address.

4. Neal McCluskey, "Run Away from 'Common' Education Standards," educationNews.org, March 18, 2010, http://www.cato.org/pub_display.php?pub_id=11609.

5. Anne L. Bryant, "NSBA Raises Concerns Tying Title I Funding to Standards Development," February 22, 2010, http://us.vocuspr.com/Newsroom/Query.aspx?SiteName=NSBANew&Entity=PRAsset&SF_PRAsset_PRAssetID_EQ=113119&XSL=PressRelease&Cache=False.

6. Catherine Gewertz, "Advocates Unite to Promote Standards' Adoption," *Education Week*, 29, no. 33 (June 9, 2010): 1, 18–19, http://www.edweek.org/ew/articles/2010/06/09/33common-strategy_ep.h29.html?qs=common+standards.

7. Robert Rothman, "Common Standards: The Time Is Now" (Washington, DC: Alliance for Excellent Education, December 2009), http://all4ed.org/files/TheTimeIsNow.pdf.

8. Campaign for High School Equity, *Communities of Color: A Critical Perspective in the Common Standards Movement* (Washington, DC: Campaign for High School Equity, nd), http://www.highschoolequity.org/images/stories/pdf/communities%20of%20color%20issue%20brief.pdf.

9. Gewertz, "Advocates Unite."

10. Opportunity Equation, "Common Core Standards: Why Did States Choose to Adopt?" Opportunityequation.org, September 21, 2010, http://opportunityequation.org/standards-and-assessments/common-core-standards-why-did-states.

11. Quoted in ibid.

12. Sheila Byrd-Carmichael, Gabrielle Martino, Kathleen Porter-Magee, and W. Stephen Wilson, *The State of State Standards—and the Common Core—in 2010* (Washington, DC: Thomas B. Fordham Institute, July 2010), http://edexcellencemedia.net/publications/2010/201007_state_education_standards_common_standards/SOSSandCC2010_FullReportFINAL.pdf.

13. National Center for Education Statistics, *The Nation's Report Card: Reading 2009* (NCES 2010-458) (Washington, DC: U.S. Department of Education, March 2010), http://nces.ed.gov/nationsreportcard/pdf/main2009/2010458.pdf.

14. National Center for Education Statistics, *The Nation's Report Card: Mathematics 2009* (NCES 2010-451) (Washington, DC: U.S. Department of Education, October 2009), http://nces.ed.gov/nationsreportcard/pdf/main2009/2010451.pdf.

15. Sandra Stotsky and Ze'ev Wurman, *Common Core's Standards Still Don't Make the Grade* (Boston: Pioneer Institute, July 2010), http://www.pioneerinstitute.org/pdf/common_core_standards.pdf.

16. "Expertise Lost at a Crucial Time," *Boston Globe*, July 29, 2010, http://www.boston.com/bostonglobe/editorial_opinion/editorials/articles/2010/07/29/expertise_lost_at_crucial_time/.

17. Byrd-Carmichael et al., *The State of State Standards*; National Center on Education Statistics, *The Nation's Report Card: Reading 2009*.

18. Byrd-Carmichael et al., *The State of State Standards*.

19. Quoted in Nick Anderson and Rosalind S. Helderman, "McDonnell Withdraws Virginia from Obama's Race to the Top School Reform Program," *Washington Post*, May 27, 2010, http://www.washingtonpost.com/wp-dyn/content/article/2010/05/26/AR2010052604480.html?nav=emailpage.

20. Quoted in Lisa Schenker, "Senate Republicans Concerned about New Academic Standards," *Salt Lake Tribune*, January 11, 2011, http://www.sltrib.com/sltrib/home/51031820-76/standards-state-utah-federal.html.csp.

21. Larry Shumway, "Defending the Common Core," utahpubliceducation.org, January 13, 2011, http://utahpubliceducation.org/2011/01/13/defending-the-common-core-initiative/.

22. Catherine Gewertz, "Local School Board in Mass. Seeks Rollback of Common Standards," *Education Week* 30, no. 19 (February 2, 2011): 6.

Chapter 6

1. Achieve, *On the Road to Implementation: Achieving the Promise of the Common Core State Standards* (Washington, DC: Achieve, August 2010).

2. Nancy Kober and Diane Stark Rentner, *State Progress and Challenges in Implementing Common Core State Standards* (Washington, DC: Center on Education Policy, January 2011).

3. Albert Shanker Institute, "A Call for Common Content: Core Curriculum Must Build a Bridge from Standards to Achievement" (Washington, DC: Albert Shanker Institute, March 2011), http://shankerinstitute.org/curriculum.html.

4. Ibid.

5. Bill Evers, Greg Forster, Jay Greene, Sandra Stotsky, and Ze'ev Wurman, "Closing the Door on Innovation: Why One National Curriculum Is Bad for America," k12innovation.com, May 2011, http://www.k12innovation.com/Manifesto/_V2_Home.html.

6. Catherine Gewirtz, "Core Knowledge to Link Curriculum to Core Standards," *Education Week* 29, no. 20 (February 3, 2010):11, http://www.edweek.org/ew/articles/2010/02/03/20standards.h29.html.

7. Catherine Gewirtz, "Gates Awards 15 Grants for Common-Standards Work," *Education Week* 29, no. 22 (February 24, 2010): 9, http://www.edweek.org/ew/articles/2010/02/18/22gates.h29.html.

8. Quoted in Catherine Gewirtz, "Gates, Pearson Partner to Craft Common-Core Curricula," *Education Week* 30, no. 30 (April 27, 2011): 1, 20, http://www.edweek.org/ew/articles/2011/04/27/30pearson.h30.html?r=2015394852.

9. Smarter Balanced Assessment Consortium, Race to the Top Assessment Program: Application for New Grants: Comprehensive Assessment System, CFDA Number 84.395B, Submitted by Washington State on Behalf of the Smarter Balanced Assessment Consortium (Olympia, WA: Washington State Department of Public Instruction, June 2011), 43.

10. MetLife Inc., *The MetLife Survey of the American Teacher: Preparing Students for College and Careers* (New York: MetLife, May 2011).

Chapter 7

1. Arne Duncan, "Beyond the Bubble Tests: The Next Generation of Assessments," remarks to the American Diploma Project Leadership Team Meeting, Washington, DC, September 2, 2010.

2. James W. Pellegrino, Naomi Chudowsky, and Robert Glaser, eds., *Knowing What Students Know: The Science and Design of Educational Assessment* (Washington, DC: National Academy Press, 2001).

3. Quoted in P. D. Chapman, *Schools as Sorters: Lewis M. Terman, Applied Psychology, and the Intelligence Testing Movement, 1890–1930* (New York: New York University Press, 1988), 33.

4. National Commission on Excellence in Education, *A Nation at Risk* (Washington, DC: U.S. Government Printing Office, 1983).

5. Joan L. Herman, "State Test Lessons: The Effects on School Reform," *Voices in Urban Education* 1 (Spring 2003): 46–55.

6. Brian Stecher and Laura Hamilton, "What Have We Learned from Pioneers in Innovative Assessment?" (paper prepared for the workshop of the Committee on Best Practices for State Assessment Systems: Improving Assessment While Revisiting Standards, National Research Council, Washington, DC, December 10–11, 2009), http://www7.nationalacademies.org/bota/Brian_Stecher_and_Laura_Hamilton.pdf.

7. Barack Obama, "Remarks of the President to the United States Hispanic Chamber of Commerce" (speech, Washington, DC, March 10, 2009).

8. Arne Duncan, "Remarks at the 2009 Governors Education Symposium" (speech, Cary, NC, June 14, 2009).

9. Linda Darling-Hammond, *Performance Counts: Assessment Systems that Support High-Quality Learning* (Washington, DC: Council of Chief State School Officers, 2010).

10. National Association of State Boards of Education, *Reform at a Crossroads: A Call for Balanced Systems of Assessment and Accountability* (Alexandria, VA: National Association of State Boards of Education, 2009), 45 (emphasis in original).

11. Alliance for Excellent Education, *Principles for a Comprehensive Assessment System* (Washington, DC: Alliance for Excellent Education, February 2010).

12. Steven Lazer, John Mazzeo, John S. Twing, Walter D. Way, Wayne Camara, and Kevin Sweeney, "Thoughts on an Assessment of Common Core Standards" (paper prepared for the U.S. Department of Education, November 16, 2009).

13. Ibid., 12.

14. U.S. Department of Education, Race to the Top Assessment Program: Notice Inviting Applications (Washington, DC: U.S. Department of Education, April 2010), 5, 6.

15. Pasquale J. DeVito, "The Oversight of State Standards and Assessment Programs: Perspectives from a Former State Assessment Director," in *Common Education Standards: Tackling the Long-Term Questions*, ed. Thomas B. Fordham Institute (Washington, DC: Thomas B. Fordham Institute, June 2010), http://www.edexcellencemedia.net/publications/2010/201006_CommonEdStandards/201006_EducationGovernance_DeVito.pdf.

16. Gregory J. Cizek, "Translating Standards into Assessments: The Opportunity and Challenges of a Common Core" (paper prepared for a symposium sponsored

by the Brookings Institution, Washington, DC, October 28, 2010), http://www
.brookings.edu/~/media/Files/events/2010/1028_race_to_the_top/1028_race_
to_the_top_cizek_paper.pdf.

17. Michael J. Feuer, Paul W. Holland, Bert F. Green, Meryl W. Bertenthal, and F.
Cadelle Hemphill, eds. *Uncommon Measures: Equivalency and Linkage among Educational Tests* (Washington, DC: National Academy Press, 1999), 5.

18. National Research Council, *State Assessment Systems: Exploring Best Practices and Innovations: Summary of Two Workshops* (Washington, DC: National Academies Press, 2010).

19. Randy Bennett, Michael Kane, and Brent Bridgeman, "Theory of Action and Validity Argument in the Context of Through-Course Summative Assessment" (paper prepared for a symposium sponsored by the Center for K–12 Assessment and Performance Management at ETS, Atlanta, February 2011).

20. Michael J. Kolen, "Generalizability and Reliability: Approaches for Through-Course Assessments" (paper prepared for a symposium sponsored by the Center for K–12 Assessment and Performance Management at ETS, Atlanta, February 2011).

21. Lauress L. Wise, "Picking up the Pieces: Aggregating Results from Through-Course Assessments" (paper prepared for a symposium sponsored by the Center for K–12 Assessment and Performance Management at ETS, Atlanta, February 2011).

22. Thomas Toch, *Margins of Error: The Education Testing Industry in the No Child Left Behind Era* (Washington, DC: Education Sector, 2006).

23. Barry Topol, John Olson, and Ed Roeber, *The Cost of New Higher Quality Assessments: A Comprehensive Analysis of the Potential Costs for Future State Assessments* (Stanford, CA: Stanford Center for Opportunity Policy in Education, 2010).

Chapter 8
1. Richard F. Elmore, "Getting to Scale with Good Educational Practice," in *School Reform from the Inside Out*, ed. R. F. Elmore (Cambridge, MA: Harvard Education Press, 2004), 11.

2. Richard Correnti and Shari Rosenberg, "Instructional Variation: Examining Differences between Populations in Variability of the Enacted Curriculum" (paper prepared for the annual meeting of the American Education Research Association, San Diego, April 2009).

3. Marshall S. Smith and Jennifer O'Day, "Systemic School Reform," in *The Politics of Curriculum and Testing: The 1990 Yearbook of the Politics of Education Association*, eds. S. H. Fuhrman and B. Malen (Bristol, PA: Falmer Press, 1991).

4. James W. Stigler and James Hiebert, *The Teaching Gap* (New York: The Free Press, 1999).

5. ACT, *A First Look at the Common Core and College and Career Readiness* (Iowa City, IA: ACT, 2010).

6. Deanna Hill, Circe Stumpo, Kathleen Paliokas, Deb Hansen, and Peter McWalters, "State Policy Implications of the Model Core Teaching Standards" (InTASC Draft Document) (Washington, DC: Council of Chief State School Officers, July 2010).

7. Mariana Haynes, *Transforming High Schools: Performance Systems for Powerful Teaching* (Washington, DC: Alliance for Excellent Education, February 2011).

8. Barnett Berry, *Teaching 2030: What We Must Do for Our Students and Our Schools, Now and in the Future* (New York: Teachers College Press, 2010).

9. Barry Topol, John Olson, and Edward Roeber, *The Cost of New Higher Quality Assessments: A Comprehensive Analysis of the Potential Costs for Future Assessments* (Stanford, CA: Stanford Center for Opportunity Policy in Education, 2010).

10. Robert Rothman, "Benchmarking and Alignment of State Standards and Assessments," in *Redesigning Accountability Systems for Education*, eds. Susan H. Fuhrman and Richard F. Elmore (New York: Teachers College Press, 2004), 96–114; Robert Rothman, Jean Slattery, Jennifer Vranek, and Lauren B. Resnick, *Benchmarking and Alignment of Standards and Testing* (Los Angeles: National Center for Research on Evaluation, Standards, and Student Testing, 2002).

11. Chester E. Finn Jr. and Michael J. Petrilli, *Now What?: Imperatives and Options for Common Core Implementation and Governance* (Washington, DC: Thomas B. Fordham Institute, October 2010).

12. Ibid, 17.

13. U.S. Department of Education, "Nation's Boldest Education Reform Plans to Receive Federal Innovation Grants Once Private Match is Secured," press release, August 5, 2010, http://www.ed.gov/news/press-releases/nations-boldest-education-reform-plans-receive-federal-innovation-grants-once-pr.

14. Frederick Hess, "Common Core vs. Charter Schooling?!! Waving that Yellow Flag," Rick Hess Straight Up, February 19, 2011, http://blogs.edweek.org/edweek/rick_hess_straight_up/2011/02/common_core_vs_charter_schooling_waving_that_yellow_flag.html.

15. Theodore R. Sizer, *Horace's School: Redesigning the American High School* (Boston: Houghton Mifflin, 1992), 111.

ABOUT THE AUTHOR

ROBERT ROTHMAN is a senior fellow at the Alliance for Excellent Education, a Washington, D.C.–based policy and advocacy organization. Previously, he was a senior editor at the Annenberg Institute for School Reform where he edited the Institute's quarterly magazine, *Voices in Urban Education*. He was also a study director at the National Research Council, where he led a committee on testing and assessment in the federal Title I program, which produced the report *Testing, Teaching, and Learning* (edited with Richard F. Elmore) and a committee on teacher testing. A nationally known education writer and editor, Mr. Rothman has also worked with Achieve and the National Center on Education and the Economy, and was a reporter and editor for *Education Week*. He has written numerous reports and articles on a wide range of education issues, and he is the editor of *City Schools* (2007) and author of *Measuring Up: Standards, Assessments and School Reform* (1995). He is also a frequent contributor to *Harvard Education Letter*. He has a degree in political science from Yale University.

INDEX